INSTRUCTOR'S RESOURCE book

by WOMEN:
AN ANTHOLOGY
of LITERATURE

Linda Heinlein Kirschner

Houghton Mifflin Company • **Boston**
Atlanta   Dallas   Geneva, Illinois   Hopewell, New Jersey   Palo Alto

ISBN: 0-395-20494-1

CONTENTS

iNTRODUCTiON

You, the classroom teacher, are faced with an exciting array of material in *By Women: An Anthology of Literature*. Here you will find selections that have not been published in any contemporary anthology. Here are familiar authors as well as writings by authors not so well known. Here are classical writers such as Sappho and Brontë and modern writers such as Wakoski and Oates. All together these writers will afford you and your students a veritable treasure of women's literature. At the same time, these writings, like any unfamiliar writing, may present an intellectual challenge. Instead of familiar works you may have taught several times and feel at home with, many of these selections will give you the opportunity to meet new writers, analyze and explicate unfamiliar works. Best of all they will offer you the chance to share with your students your enthusiasm for women's literature. Such a sharing is, indeed, an exciting and challenging prospect.

This manual has been prepared as an aid to you. It is hoped that you will find the material helpful in your own study of women's literature. The answers to the questions asked in both the text and manual are not meant to be definitive. They represent one impression, one point of view, one interpretation. Perhaps the comments may serve as a point of departure for further discussion or perhaps they may serve as a point of argument. They will, it is hoped, help you in leading your students to an enthusiastic appreciation for women's literature. Similarly, the books listed in Suggested Reading are meant to aid you as you guide your students' reading. The selections marked with an asterisk are appropriate for the average reader while other selections will be especially effective with your more sophisticated readers. After examining the suggested readings, you will be the best guide in helping your students expand their knowledge for you know your students, their abilities, and their interests. Finally, it is hoped that the material in both the text and the manual will help you in guiding your students toward a keener understanding of women's literature, of women, and of themselves.

Short Stories

The Story of an Hour / p. 3
Kate Chopin (1851–1904)

Kate Chopin wrote of the conflict women can feel over their desire to be wives and mothers and their need to be self-assertive individuals. Her stories and novels often deal with the woman who awakens to herself and is freed from societal and personal restraints. In "The Story of an Hour" Mrs. Mallard, when informed of her husband's death, experiences a sense of overwhelming freedom and joy at her release from years of repression. Ironically, her "story" lasts for only an hour before she dies from what the doctor describes as a "joy that kills."

Insight

1. The freedom means that she would no longer be bound in a relationship that imposed "a private will upon a fellow-creature." She will be free to live for herself, to enjoy the days as she alone desires. It means being fully herself—"this possession of self-assertion which she suddenly recognized as the strongest impulse of her being" (page 4).

   Some students may see Mrs. Mallard as a selfish person whose feelings at her husband's death are unnatural. However, even those students will probably sympathize with her desire for freedom and self-assertion, a desire they themselves have undoubtedly felt.

   Other students will see Mrs. Mallard as a woman who has been a good wife, but who has had her will bent by one more powerful in the "blind persistence which men and women believe they have a right to impose" (page 4). It is not selfishness that Kate Chopin wants the reader to see, but the powerful, human impulse for independence and self-assertion.

2. Mrs. Mallard's sister and friend are afraid that she will have a heart attack when she hears of her husband's death. Instead she has the fatal attack when she discovers that he is alive after all. The shock of having her new-found freedom snatched away is too much for her. There is further irony in that the others think she has died of joy from seeing her husband alive, when she has really died of shock and despair.

Additional Questions

1. Chopin states that Mrs. Mallard's reaction to the news of her husband's death differs from that of most women. What might this indicate about Mrs. Mallard as a person and about her relationship with her husband? What hints are we given about that relationship?

   The Mallards appear to have had a superficially happy marriage, with Mr. Mallard showing only love and tenderness toward his wife. But any

1

desires for self-assertion and freedom on Mrs. Mallard's part had been so deeply repressed over the years that even she had no hint of their existence. In his own kind and loving way, Mr. Mallard had completely subjugated his wife's will to his own.

2. After weeping over her husband's death, Mrs. Mallard returns to her room alone. What does she see as she looks out the window, and how does the scene reflect her awakening sense of freedom?

   She sees an open square filled with "new spring life" and a "delicious breath of rain." There are patches of blue sky in the clouds. It is a description of rebirth, of life, of vitality, that is soon repeated in her recognition of the joy that is sweeping over her.

Composition

Describe an ironic situation that happened in your life or that you know about. In your description, make clear the incongruity between what was expected to happen and what actually happened, or between what was thought to be true and what turned out to be true. If you cannot think of an ironic situation that actually happened, make one up.

The Sentimentality of William Tavener / p. 6
Willa Cather (1873–1947)

Although Hester and William Tavener have made a prosperous life for themselves in the West, it was not done easily or without damage to their own relationship. Like the Taveners, Willa Cather moved West from her Virginia birthplace to a Nebraska ranch. There on the lonely plains, she became a part of the land and its people, whose harshness and beauty she so vividly describes in her writing.

Insight

1. The boys feel they have lost an ally because until now she has always been on their side. "No debtor ever haggled with his usurer more doggedly than did Hester with her husband in behalf of her sons" (page 9). At the end of the story, however, it is William who receives her protective gestures and the boys who are shown her sharpness. Hester has switched her primary allegiance to her husband, and the boys realize this.

2. The change in Hester is that she no longer sees herself as William's business partner but as a tender and protective wife. Their exchange of confidences had opened both their hearts and "had all the miracle of romance" (page 9). The rediscovery of warmth and closeness makes her realize that she had missed something, that "somehow the years had cheated her" (page 9).

3. As Hester and William rediscover their former closeness, the tone of the story becomes increasingly affectionate and nostalgic. This tone is expressed by such expressions as "miracle of romance," "old familiar faces," "long forgotten incidents." By the end of the story the tone is one of tenderness and regret as Cather describes Hester's "painful sense of having missed something."

Additional Questions

1. Hester and William Tavener both have strong personalities. How are they described in the story?

   Hester is described as a "good manager" and "an executive woman" who is bossy and determined to have her way. She is portrayed as warm toward her sons, if businesslike with her husband. She has an air of nagging shrewishness, but in her outspoken manner there is directness and honesty. She is a hard-working, vigorous woman. Cather describes William as "hard" and "grasping, determined and ambitious." He is grave and silent, using silence as a protection. But both of them have hidden qualities of warmth and "sentimentality" which are rediscovered in their exchange of confidences.

2. Why, do you think, Cather called the story "The Sentimentality of William Tavener"?

   The title emphasizes that the key event of the story is the revelation of William's unsuspected "sentimentality." It is this revelation that causes Hester to see him and herself in an entirely different light and leads them to rediscover a close and tender relationship which had been lost.

Composition

Choose a real or imaginary character to describe. Write two descriptions of the person. In the first, make it clear by the tone that you dislike the character. In the second, make it clear by the tone that you like the character very much. In both cases do not state directly that you like or dislike the character. Remember that tone is expressed by choice of words and selection of details and by emphasis and comments that are made.

The Jilting of Granny Weatherall / p. 11
Katherine Anne Porter (born 1894)

At the end of a long life, surrounded by her loving children, Granny Weatherall should be filled with happy memories. Instead, a long-rankling hurt revolves in her fading mind and leads to the pain of her dying moments. Here, as in so many of her stories, Porter captures the essence of human feeling and motivation.

Insight

1. The technique is effective because it conveys the vagueness of Granny's mind and the confusion between past and present that is common to old people. Also, as her mind shifts between past and present we learn about her entire life. Granny thinks of her jilting, her subsequent marriage, her children, the years of hard work. She remembers her readiness for death when she was sixty, but is aware of her lack of preparation for it at eighty. But most of all, again and again, she returns to thoughts of George and his jilting of her. Granny's thoughts reveal the successful, hard life of a strong, capable woman—but a woman who has remained vulnerable over the years because of one terrible hurt.
2. The grief is that she has received no sign from God that she has been accepted and saved. When she receives no sign, it is as if she has been jilted again. The second rejection is much more devastating than the first because it comes after a lifetime of expectation.

Additional Questions

1. Describe the events in the jilting of Granny Weatherall by her fiancé.
   As a young woman dressed in her white veil with the white cake ready to cut, Granny had waited on her wedding day for George, her fiancé. When it became obvious that he was not coming, "the whole bottom dropped out of the world" (page 17). She had nearly fainted, but John had caught her before she fell. Cursing, John had said, "I'll kill him for you." It was this same John whom she later married and who made her a good husband.
2. The major portion of Granny's life occurs between the first jilting and the final jilting. Would you say that her life has been a happy and satisfying one?
   Most students will feel she has had a satisfying and productive life. She has certainly taken pride in her accomplishments and until the end has not dwelled upon her first love. She was a good wife and mother and carried on the work of the farm after her husband's death. Other students will feel Granny has been superficially happy but "for sixty years she had prayed against remembering him and against losing her soul in the deep pit of hell" (page 14). She has done her best to find happiness, but the wound of rejection has never totally healed.
3. Notice Granny's last name. What significance does it have to the story?
   One meaning of "weather" is to endure, to come through safely. In her long life Granny has encountered many hardships and obstacles, and she has weathered them all.

Composition

Chose an incident from the past, either true or imaginary. Write a stream-of-consciousness passage in which you slowly reveal the truth about that event, as Porter has done in "The Jilting of Granny Weatherall."

The Demon Lover / p. 20
Elizabeth Bowen (1899–1973)

Promising to return someday, a mysterious soldier departs for a war in which he is eventually declared missing, presumed dead. Could he really expect a woman to wait twenty-five years? During another war Mrs. Drover returns briefly to her London home never expecting the consequences of the "sinister troth" made so long ago. Elizabeth Bowen, with her sensitivity to details of time, place, and atmosphere, creates here an eerie, disquieting tale.

Insight

1. There is about the London house a closed, hollow atmosphere. The rain makes the house darker and drearier than Mrs. Drover remembered it. It is, for example, "dead air [that] came out to meet her as she went in" (page 20). Mrs. Drover, long used to hearing familiar family voices in the house that had always been open to sunlight and warmth, is considerably affected by the present atmosphere. She feels ill at ease, disoriented, almost as if it were not her own home.

2. Perhaps the most important detail we learn of her past is her short relationship with the soldier. She was certainly not in command of that situation, was afraid of him and of the "sinister troth" they pledged. Now in the midst of another war she experiences the same feeling of dislocation that she felt upon hearing of her soldier's death so long ago. Her present state of mind is one of nervousness and uncertainty. In the midst of the familiar, she feels disoriented and afraid.

Additional Questions

1. The title of the story is taken from the following well-known old English ballad by the same name:

The Demon Lover

"Oh, where have you been, my long, long love,
    This long seven years and more?"
"Oh, I've come to seek my former vows
    Ye granted me before."

"Oh, do not speak of your former vows,   5
    For they will breed sad strife;
Oh, do not speak of your former vows,
    For I have become a wife."

He turned him right and round about,
    And the tear blinded his ee: 10

"I would never have trodden on this ground
    If it had not been for thee."

"If I was to leave my husband dear,
    And my two babes also,
Oh, what have you to take me to,   15
    If with you I should go?"

"I have seven ships upon the sea—
    The eighth brought me to land—
With four-and-twenty bold mariners,
    And music on every hand."   20

She has taken up her two little babes,
    Kissed them on cheek and chin:
"Oh, fare ye well, my own two babes,
    For I'll never see you again."

She set her foot upon the ship—   25
    No mariners could she behold;
But the sails were of the taffeta,
    And the masts of the beaten gold.

She had not sailed a league, a league,
    A league but barely three,   30
When dismal grew his countenance,
    and drumlie* grew his ee.

They had not sailed a league, a league,
    A league but barely three,
Until she espied his cloven foot,   35
    And she wept right bitterly.

"Oh, hold your tongue of your weeping," said he,
    "Of your weeping now let me be;
I will show you how the lilies grow
    On the banks of Italy."   40

"Oh, what hills are yon, yon pleasant hills,
    That the sun shines sweetly on?"
"Oh, yon are the hills of heaven," he said,
    "Where you will never win."

"Oh, whaten a mountain is yon," she said,   45
    "So dreary with frost and snow?"
"Oh, yon is the mountain of hell," he cried,
    "Where you and I will go."

[32] DRUMLIE: dark.

He struck the top-mast with his hand,
  The fore-mast with his knee;   50
And he broke that gallant ship in twain,
  And sank her in the sea.

Compare the tone of the ballad with that of the story. What atmosphere is created in both selections? What effect does this atmosphere have upon the action of the story?

In both the ballad and the story there is a grim, somber tone unrelieved by any humor. Mrs. Drover, looking back on her brief relationship remembers that the soldier "was set on me." The lover in the ballad leaves us with the same impression as he says, "I've come to seek my former vows" (line 3).

2. Bowen has written, "Willing though we are to be moved and held, none of us can be held by the unbelievable." In what ways is "The Demon Lover" illustrative of this statement?

As eerie as they may seem, both the specific events of the day and the general atmosphere of a bombed-out city are at the same time believable. The story is set in the gloom of any rainy day, and Mrs. Drover could be any rather nervous woman returning to a long-closed house. The prosaic elements of this all too believable setting move and hold the reader.

3. Ghost stories or tales of the supernatural are most effective when elements of reality are combined with elements of disbelief. In "The Demon Lover" these two are mixed most effectively. What supernatural elements are present in the story? What elements of reality? Would you classify this as a ghost story? Or do you feel it is more a story of a psychotic woman? Explain.

The letter appearing on the table, the spectral quality of her lover, the draft emanating from the basement, the taxi driver's behavior, might all be seen as examples of the supernatural. At the same time, some students will give reasons to view these as realistic happenings.

Composition

Choose a setting you know well and describe it in a way that makes it seem frightening and sinister.

Death of a Traveling Salesman / p. 26
Eudora Welty (born 1909)

Years of being on the road take their toll on R. J. Bowman as a lifetime of accumulated frustration and loneliness finally catches up with him. In her clear, compressed style, Eudora Welty portrays the alienated individual as he comes to the realization that his life is empty and loveless.

Insight

1. The illness has left him weak and tired and has made him question his way of life. Until then he had been so busy that he could avoid thinking about his real situation in life. Now he realizes how empty and lonely his life is. When he arrives at the house, he is exhausted from the long, hot drive, his heart is acting up, and he is desperate for solace and rest.

2. Bowman feels a "curious and strong emotion" (page 32) toward the woman. He has a barely controllable urge to embrace her. He wants to invite her into his heart, which is struggling in protest against emptiness. Then he feels ashamed that he came so close to communicating "some strange thing—something which seemed always to have just escaped him" (page 33). Later he watches with resentment and anger as she moves away from him and toward Sonny. "From what was he being deprived? His chest was rudely shaken by the violence of his heart. These people cherished something here that he could not see, they withheld some ancient promise of food and warmth and light" (page 34).

3. The realization is overwhelming because it throws into unbearable contrast his own barren, loveless life. He sees that they have everything he has missed. What makes the bleakness of his life even more unbearable is his belief that a fruitful marriage is a simple thing that anyone could have had. Whether or not a fruitful marriage is indeed a simple thing that anyone can have is beside the point; the important thing is that Bowman *believes* it is a simple thing. Therefore, what he must face is this: his life is empty and loveless and apparently unalterably so, but it could have easily been otherwise. Facing up to that realization is too much for him; the pain of it kills him.

4. In this story the personal point of view is used. The story is told through the eyes of the central character, who is referred to in the third person. We see everything through Bowman's eyes; we know nothing except what Bowman himself sees or thinks or hears.

   The advantage of using the personal point of view is that the truth about the couple is revealed to the reader at the same time that Bowman himself learns it. If the reader knew beforehand, it would blunt the effect of the discovery, which is the key event of the story. By telling the story through Bowman's eyes, Welty allows the reader to share his experience of shocked revelation.

   In the last line of the story the point of view shifts to an outside observer who notes "But nobody heard it." The sudden shift from Bowman's consciousness indicates that his consciousness has ceased, that he is dead. The shift is necessary because with the personal point of view there is no way to indicate the character's death except by a shift in point of view or by use of metaphor (as in "she . . . blew out the light" at the end of "The Jilting of Granny Weatherall").

Composition

Choose one scene from the story and retell it from the point of view of the woman in the story. You may use either the first or third person—that is, the woman can tell the story directly using "I," or she can be referred to in the third person. In either case, remember that with the personal point of view the reader knows only what that particular character thinks, feels, does, and observes. For instance, the woman would know nothing about Bowman except what he tells her and what she can observe.

By the North Gate / p. 39
Joyce Carol Oates (born 1938)

The deeper philosophical meaning of this complex story may elude some readers. However, most people will undoubtedly respond to the atmosphere of the story and its emotional impact. The prolific, award-winning writer Joyce Carol Oates skillfully captures the essence of life as it has been experienced by old man Revere.

Insight

1. Some of the passages that might be mentioned are the following: (a) The first line of the story: "The first time something strange happened to him. . . ." (b) "He knew before he woke that something strange had happened. Maybe in the house, maybe outside. And, later, as he groped around in the near dark . . . he heard the hound whining" (page 39). It was then that he had discovered the dog's ears had been slit. (c) The scene in which a fire was mysteriously set in the grass field by the barn, beginning "Somehow the sight of the white smoke rising slowly . . ." (page 40). (d) The farmer by the schoolhouse who used to say, "You watch out life don't catch up with you" (page 42). Then the farmer would seem to forget Revere. "His hands would be busy pulling absently and viciously at stalks of grass growing by the fence posts, pulling them out and shredding them in his strong fingers, and letting the wind blow the pieces away" (page 43). (e) The paragraph beginning "Then Revere woke with a start" (page 46). (f) The scene with the boys when they come asking for water, which begins on page 46. "Revere was angry his heart was pounding so. . . . The boy was smiling in a broad, peculiar way"; in fact all three boys have peculiar smiles. Later Revere "saw with a strange, weakening sense of dismay—a sense of something within him dissolving, collapsing—that they had no bottles or buckets. . . ." (g) The sense of foreboding reaches its height when the boys are walking away, then turn and call, "You got yourself some flies there" (page 48). The reader may even realize what has happened before Revere himself knows it.

These suggestions of strangeness and impending evil create an atmosphere of menacing evil, of threatening confusion, of almost unbearable suspense. Most students will feel a strong sense of foreboding and tension as they read the story.

2. When his dog's ears are slit, Revere wants to know *why* it has happened. "He knew that something had happened. And there had to be a reason for it—a reason he must try to discover. He had always had faith in understanding and knowledge, the kind of thinking found in books" (page 41). When the boys kill the dog his reaction is again an anguished "Why did you do that?" He chases after them, not to punish them, but to ask why they have done it. Again and again he shouts, "Why did you?" Desperately he struggles against seeing the incident as a judgment on life, that life is meaningless evil. "All my life I done battle against it, that life don't mean nothin'! . . . You ain't goin' to change my mind now, an' me grown so old an' come so far . . ." (page 49).

   Then, by an exhausting effort of will, he sees the boys as "caught within the accidental pattern of a fate in which he himself would be caught" (page 49). The boys are just boys; their action does not mean the world is evil and meaningless. "They don't stand for anything s'post to change my mind about life."

3. One possible answer is that the memory of the scene in the schoolhouse comforts him because it represents reason and understanding—the world of books and the knowledge they contain. Even though he himself may not know the answer, it comforts him to believe that an answer exists somewhere. In discussing a story of magic, Revere had said "It don't make no sense 'cause things don't happen that way in the world" (page 50). Revere cannot remember the teacher's answer, but what he can remember—the smell of chalk and dust and so forth—is a comfort to him. The memory is like the clear light of reason and order that cuts through the confused mists of his own limited understanding.

4. Oates develops Revere's character primarily through showing what goes on inside his head—his memories and his thoughts about what is happening to him. Also we learn about him from the way other people treat him and how he reacts to their treatment. Oates uses the personal point of view in the story, and she makes no direct comments about his character. Everything we learn in the story is through Revere's consciousness.

   Revere is an inarticulate man of limited intelligence. He cannot express in words either his feelings or his thoughts. In the scene with his daughter Nancy, when his wife was dying, he cannot speak. "Revere's face ached as if it wanted to smile or something, but when he opened his mouth to talk he had nothing to say" (page 45). His inability to communicate makes him feel as if people are always strangers to one another. He frequently feels confused and ashamed. Yet there is a kind of simple nobility in his fierce struggle to believe that life has meaning. He has a moral courage that enables him to endure the "picking torment" and failures of his life without losing his faith.

Composition

Choose a character to describe, either real or imaginary. Decide what the character's most important qualities are—courage, cruelty, humor, kindness, deceitfulness, whatever. Then write a passage about the character showing those qualities without actually naming them. You may find that once you get started, you can expand the passage into a complete story.

In Summary

There is about the short story a marvelous, compact microcosm of life. Characters develop; conflict appears; resolution occurs. Throughout the action, no matter what time or what place, a voice is telling us a tale, sharing a moment with us. The story thus becomes a starting point toward an insight into some particular aspect of human existence. How many of us, after all, have experienced a jilting so filled with anguish that the loss influences our daily lives and haunts our dying day? Yet, through a short story of Granny Weatherall's last moments, we share her anguish, feel her keen loss. Her life, and perhaps a small piece of our own, becomes a bit easier to comprehend.

It is important to realize that the short story writer has accomplished a single purpose, has created a single impression. She has had to write compactly and concisely. All extraneous matter must be deleted so that one single impression is achieved. The study of character, of setting, of mood, of conflict is vital to the understanding of the story itself, for it is these elements of the story that in the end unite to create the single effect essential to every story.

Suggested Reading

*Buck, Pearl. *The Good Earth*. New York: John Day, 1965.
*Bowen, Elizabeth. *Early Stories*. New York: Alfred A. Knopf, 1951.
———. *Ivy Gripped the Steps*. New York: Alfred A. Knopf, 1946.
*Cather, Willa. *My Antonia*. Boston: Houghton Mifflin, 1961.
———. *Obscure Destinies*. New York: Alfred A. Knopf, 1932.
———. *The Old Beauty and Others*. New York: Alfred A. Knopf, 1948.
Chopin, Kate. *The Awakening and Other Stories*. L. Leary, ed. New York: Holt, Rinehart & Winston, 1970.
Gallant, Mavis. *The Pegnitz Junction: A Novella and Five Short Stories*. New York: Random House, 1973.

Grau, Shirley A. *The Black Prince and Other Stories*. New York: Alfred A. Knopf, 1965.

*Jackson, Shirley. *The Magic of Shirley Jackson*. Stanley Edgar Hyman, ed. New York: Farrar Straus & Giroux, 1966.

Lagerlof, Selma. *Marbacka*. Howard Velma, Ann Arbor, Mich.: Finch Press, 1926.

Lavin, Mary. *Collected Stories*. Boston: Houghton Mifflin, 1971.

Oates, Joyce Carol. *By the North Gate*. New York: Vanguard Press, 1963.

O'Brien, Edna. *Casualties of Peace*. Simon and Schuster, 1967.

*Parker, Dorothy. *The Portable Dorothy Parker*. New York: Viking Press, 1973.

Porter, Katherine Anne. *Flowering Judas and Other Stories*. New York: Random House, 1930.

———. *Pale Horse, Pale Rider*. New York: Harcourt, Brace and World, 1936.

*Stafford, Jean. *Bad Characters*. New York: Farrar Straus & Giroux, 1964.

———. *Collected Stories*. New York: Farrar Straus & Giroux, 1969.

Taylor, Elizabeth. *Dedicated Man and Other Stories*. New York: Viking Press, 1965.

Welty, Eudora. *Selected Short Stories of Eudora Welty*. New York: Random House, 1954.

———. *Wide Net and Other Stories*. New York: Harcourt, Brace and World, 1943.

*Wharton, Edith. *Ethan Frome*. New York: Scribner's, 1911.

———. *Roman Fever and Other Stories*. Scribner's, 1964.

———. *House of Mirth*. New York: Holt, Rinehart & Winston, 1964.

Search for Self

Portrait of Girl with Comic Book / p. 55
Phyllis McGinley (born 1905)

Nikki-Roasa / p. 56
Nikki Giovanni (born 1943)

Phyllis McGinley defines here that in-between age of thirteen as it is seen from an adult's point of view. Nikki Giovanni, on the other hand, reflects upon her own youth and realizes that it will be hard for others to "understand that all the while I was quite happy."

Insight

1. Many students will agree that the most negative aspect of being thirteen is the fact that you are not yet an adult. You are not old enough for face powder, "or misses' clothing,/Or intellect, or grace" (lines 4–5). Other students may feel that the loss of childhood is the most negative aspect of being thirteen. You are, for example, too old for dolls and too old to play with cars. Certainly the age is full of ambivalences such as being afraid, but not admitting it, wanting nothing and at the same time wanting everything, having best friends that you hate.

2. Giovanni portrays her childhood with an attitude of intensity and satisfaction. She asserts that she may not have had an inside toilet or a fancy bathtub, but she did have her mother all to herself and attended family meetings with the whole family. Her father might have drunk too much and her parents fought a lot, but a least "everybody is together" (line 22) and holidays were celebrated with joy, and there was a lot of love.

3. Although both poems deal with the subject of childhood, the McGinley poem treats the subject in a lighter vein. This poem, more an impersonal characterization of an age, defines the age in terms of what it is not. The Giovanni poem, on the other hand, is a more personal, more intense poem. Reflecting on her own childhood, the speaker is defending it from biographers and white persons who might assess those years as unhappy ones.

Additional Question

"Thirteen's anomalous" (line 17) remarks the speaker in the McGinley poem. What does the poem suggest is anomalous about this age? Could the word anomalous be used to describe any elements of the Giovanni poem? Explain.

"Thirteen's anomalous" because it is between childhood and adulthood, and as a result, it cannot be defined or described in terms of either age. It "is the one age defeats the metaphor." In the Giovanni poem, the view of

13

childhood is anomalous to her biographer's view or perhaps to a white person's view. Giovanni feels that people will not understand that because she was poor, she was not emotionally deprived of love or happiness.

from The Diary of Anaïs Nin / p. 58
Anaïs Nin (born 1903)

"I have wanted in my writing to unmask the deeper self that lies hidden behind the self that we present to the world," Anais Nin once commented. It is the self the world sees and a mirror reflects, as well as the deeper, hidden self that Nin examines in this section from her diary.

Insight

1. First, Nin sees herself as a character from her imagination, a Marie Antoinette or a Joan of Arc. This purely romantic image is not of herself at all. However, in the next mirrored reflection, the image of self has become more evident. The self now is a girl with frightened eyes, an insecure child ashamed of her meager clothes. In the next reflection, however, the frightened child is replaced by a less realistic image. The reflection now "is never Anaïs Nin who goes to school, and grows vegetables and flowers in her backyard" (page 60). It is instead, impersonations of famous and beautiful women. The final reflection at sixteen proves to the narrator that the mirror holds no answers. "She will have to look for the answer in the eyes and faces of the boys who dance with her, men later, and above all the painters" (page 60).
2. Nin contends that children never really see themselves in a mirror. They see a child but the image is actually meaningless to them. She asserts that children are too busy with their feelings, with their emotions, to be concerned with their physical being. In her own case as a child, Nin never saw herself in the mirror. Instead she romantically saw views of herself as Joan of Arc or Charlotte Corday or some other legendary figure.

Additional Question

Do you agree with Nin's evaluation that "perhaps a child, like a cat, is so much inside of himself that he does not see himself in the mirror?" (page 58). Is it possible that some adults may also fit this statement?

Some students may well agree that children, so full of themselves, are unable to look outside of themselves and to view themselves realistically. It might be suggested that this ability comes only with maturity and even immature adults are not able to see themselves as they really are. Other students may feel that even young children see their own images and accept the image they see. These students may suggest that what is seen is dependent upon the viewer's personality. Romantic people may always see someone else in a mirror, just as Nin has done. Practical people may never see anything but themselves reflected.

Composition

Study your own reflection in a mirror. How would you describe what you see? How close to your actual self do you think your perception is?

The New Mirror / p. 61
Ann Petry (born 1912)

A few moments spent in front of a new mirror profoundly affect the lives of a girl and her father in this warm story of family pride and love.

Insight

1. The narrator is a fifteen-year-old girl of unusual perceptions and maturity. She enjoys helping the family in the drugstore, and when left in charge, she acts with maturity and displays a keen sense of responsibility. Seen in relationship with family members, particularly her father, it is clear that she is a thinking person, one who analyzes and attempts to evaluate her emotions and feelings. She obviously loves her father deeply, although she is somewhat critical of his physical appearance. His toothlessness has bothered her for a long time, but her many hints about false teeth have been ignored. Like her father, she is also imaginative. She would like to believe the tree really does talk to her father; the idea intrigues her imagination. Although her mature self recognizes the foolishness, she will later go to the yard and listen to the tree and bees. "As I stood there, I felt it would be very easy to believe that those trees could speak to me" (page 68).

2. Both the father and the daughter have a new perception of themselves as they look in the new mirror with its bright light. The daughter becomes intensely dissatisfied with her long braid "because it was an absolutely revolting hair style for a fifteen-year-old girl" (page 61). Her dark skin is not the color brown she wishes; she is "too big, too dark." Because of the new mirror the father decides to get false teeth. The mirror emphasizes "the open mouth all red and moist inside, and the naked gums with a tooth here and there, and it was the mouth of an idiot out of Shakespeare, it was the mouth of the nurse in *Romeo and Juliet*, the mouth of the gravediggers in *Hamlet* . . ." (page 81).

3. The Layens, the only black family in a white community, must feel constantly on guard and on display. They very carefully act with propriety in their store and on the street. But in their own home, away from the public eye, they speak and act as they please. This is their private life. It is the only part of their life away from the scrutiny of others, and as a result the narrator feels it is their weapon, their secret,

hidden from the town's or the enemy's view. Implied in the feeling is their alienation from others, from everyone else around them. Certainly the women in the family, as they try to find Mr. Layen, parallel this metaphor of the family against the enemy. The work of the drugstore goes on as usual with everyone attempting to give a sense of normality. People are even escorted to the door as usual, just as if Mr. Layen were there himself. Even the daughter, so imbued in the spirit of putting on a public face, carefully explains to the police that her father has found his watch, not that he himself had been considered lost.

4. Samuel was damned because he has no teeth and looks like a typical stereotyped image of Uncle Tom. And if he has new teeth, he again is stereotyped, this time as the happy black man, "white teeth flashing in a black and grinning face." The daughter realizes that no matter what action she takes, whether she honestly explains her father's disappearance or lies about it, she, too, is "damned." To be honest will be to confirm other's, especially the white townspeople's opinions of the family. To lie is to damn herself. Her pride in herself, in her very blackness as she looks at the skin of her hand against the white notepaper, is what gives her the strength to say that her father had returned and had found his watch. A small lie told to save the family's pride as well as her own.

Additional Questions

1. To what extent do the events of the story revolve around the fact that the Layens are a black family? Support your answer with specific references to the story. How might the story have developed had the family been white?

   Some students will suggest that it is not necessary for the family to be black. They may say that any family with a sense of pride might well react to events as this family did. Other students will suggest that the Layen's pride results from their being black, particularly black in an all-white community. They might well have acted differently had they lived in a community in which they were in the majority. As it is, their behavior in the drugstore, their attitude in notifying the police, their unwillingness to share their problem with anyone, even their refusal to look on the street for Samuel are all a result of their feeling alienated from their community. And this alienation is solely a result of their race. Some students might further suggest that had the family been white, the story could well have climaxed with a scene in which the townspeople seek Samuel together.

2. What is the significance of relating the Layens' arrival in Albany to the story as a whole? In what way does the narrator's echo of the words, "You ain't taking us back now," (page 74) symbolize her actions and attitude?

The incredible pride of these people, of the parents and grandparents of Samuel, is evident from the incident recounted. One can easily understand where Samuel found his own sense of pride and where, in turn, as the daughter is faced with talking to the police, she found her sense of pride. Like her ancestors, she is not about to go "back."

3. In what way do the blossoming cherry trees and the humming bees add to the overall mood of the story?

The mood of the story is one of warmth and life. The cherry trees and the bees exude this same feeling. Certainly the family is a warm, tight-knit family that stands alone, isolated from their community even while they serve it. Without bitterness or anger, Petry tells a story of life, and warmth, and a tremendous sense of pride.

Composition

Describe an incident from your own life in which pride determined your course of behavior. To what extent were you aware at the time of what was motivating you?

In Mind / p. 84
Denise Levertov (born 1923)

Mirror / p. 86
Sylvia Plath (1932–1963)

The Double Goer / p. 87
Dilys Laing (1906–1960)

Learning who we are and realizing the possibilities of who we could be, represent two of the most important objectives of a human life. Three modern poets speak eloquently and poignantly on this universal theme.

Insight

1. Although now aging, the woman in "Mirror" once was a young girl with the vanity and tensions of most young girls. Now she turns her back on the truthful mirror and uses candles and moonlight to mask her aging years. The woman in "The Double Goer" is also aging, and as she does so, her dissatisfaction with herself, who she is, and where she is going, grows. Because she needs a change from herself, she journeys to find a new self, a more satisfying self. The woman in "In Mind" is also searching for an identity, but she sees there are two persons within her from which to choose. She can be the natural, innocent, simple woman with no imagination or she can be the turbulent, imaginative woman who "is not kind" (line 17). The details given about the women in these three poems clarify the conflicts raised in each poem.

In each case, an identity is being searched for, an escape from one's present self is being sought.

2. Attempting to deny her identity, the woman in "Mirror" does not resignedly accept her aging vision. She continues to ease her image with candles and moonlight, and as the mirror says, "she rewards me with tears and an agitation of hands" (line 14). The woman in "In Mind" defined two personalities from which she could choose, yet she has not made her decision. It is the woman in "The Double Goer" who has most clearly identified herself. Because of her intense personal dissatisfactions, she has sought a new identity, but unable to escape her old identity, she returns to it.

Additional Question

"Mirror" and "The Double Goer" both deal with growing older. What attitude toward aging do these two poems appear to present? Which poem presents a more hopeful picture of aging? Explain.

Both poems show women unhappy and fearful with the process of aging. Neither woman can accept the process. To the woman in "The Double Goer," the fifty years of her life have taken her nowhere. She is dissatisfied and wants to accomplish something. Even though she is unable to satisfy her sense of identity, she is loved and cared for anyway. In "Mirror" there is a less hopeful attitude toward aging. The imagery of lines 17–18 ". . . and in me an old woman/Rises toward her day after day, like a terrible fish," appears to coincide with the woman's sense of disaster as she watches her reflection age.

Samuel / p. 89
Grace Paley (born 1922)

In this short story Grace Paley examines the actions of the "brave" and the "watchful" individuals as they come into conflict with one another.

Insight

1. Students will probably point out that the men who had been brave boys themselves watch these boys with benign amusement and recall daring moments from their own youth. The antics of these boys look less risky than their own remembered exploits. But to the man "whose boyhood had been more watchful than brave" these boys and their behavior create only anger, and he pulls the emergency cord. Students may suggest that one tends to react as one has been brought up to react. Thus, those who were brought up to be "brave" will find pride in similar behavior while those taught to be "watchful" will be wary of the brave and will fear those who threaten their own watchfulness.

2. Paley's very use of the word "brave" in connection with the behavior of the boys is one hint that she does not disapprove of Samuel's behavior.

Certainly the last paragraph implies that Samuel was special for "never again will a boy exactly like Samuel be known" (page 91). It was his braveness, his eagerness to prove himself, to be a part of the action, that set him apart. Although the "watchful" of the world may be many, their accomplishments are few, for they do not dare to act as the "brave" do. At least, as Paley implies in this story, to be "brave" is to have dared to try.

Additional Question

How do the women on the train react to the boys? In what way do their feelings after Samuel's death differ from those of the men?

The women would apparently all belong to the "watchful" classification for they all become angry and upset with the boys' behavior as does the "watchful" man. The one woman who takes action parallels the behavior of the one man who takes action in that both are interested in removing the boys from the danger. After Samuel's death, the men return to their memories of "other afternoons with very bad endings" while the women worry about Samuel's mother and whether she has another child to take Samuel's place.

Composition

Which group of people in the world do you feel is more to be admired, the "brave" or the "watchful"? What dangers are inherent in each group? How would you classify yourself?

My First Two Women / p. 92
Nadine Gordimer (born 1923)

This psychological tale of a young boy growing up under the influence of two mothers, neither of whom gives him the maternal love he seeks, is convincingly told by the South African writer Nadine Gordimer.

Insight

1. Students will probably point out that the young boy's feelings for his absentee mother were vague and undefined. He was eager to please her when she expected certain behavior from him, and he enjoyed being with her. However, she was not, at that point, a particularly important influence upon him and as a result, his relationship with her was not central to his existence. After Deb's arrival the young boy learned to "use" his mother as a liberating force in his life. Because hers was a glamorous and free life, and his father's and Deb's a more disciplined, ordinary existence, the boy would often compare their ways of living and imply that life was better with his real mother. He learned he could exert a special power over Deb by invoking his mother's world. "... That power ... had come to me like a set of magical weapons ... I

crushed upon my little-boy's head the vainglory and triumph of the tyrant, crown or thorn. I was to wear it as my own for the rest of my childhood" (page 99). By the end of the story, his view of his mother is more realistic. Neither ignoring her, nor using her to gain his own ends, he now sees her realistically as a woman "rather fleshy" who "sings off-key" (page 103). Certainly the young boy never, even from early childhood, saw his mother in a particularly maternal role. She was more simply a woman in his life, a woman whose usefulness to him was important, but whose love was lacking.

2. The boy's mother had her world, her friends, and her travels all of which consumed her interest. The boy was a fascination to her, but more as a showpiece or a novelty. She would cut his hair like her own and enjoy the comments of her friends, but her maternal feelings for her son never appeared deep.

3. On at least two occasions, the young boy's subconscious pleads with Deb to be his mother. "I'm your second mother," (page 95) she responds initially hoping perhaps not to be forced into denying his first mother. Deb's response to his statement that he loved her best was one of joy. Yet, because Deb had earlier agreed with her husband that they would never try to supplant the boy's real mother, she is now caught in the difficult situation of wanting to be his mother, being awkwardly joyful at being asked, yet not being able to accept the coveted role.

4. The young boy needs the love, tenderness, and acceptance of one person. He wants one mother to love and to care for him, not two women, neither of whom ever completely fulfills his needs. Deb, on the other hand, emotionally wishes to be this mother to the young boy, but rationally decides to withhold a portion of herself for his sake. As a result, the boy suffers and Deb suffers, and they are never more than just friends. "It was true: that was what we were — all we were" (page 103). And the boy concludes, "I have never forgiven her for it" (page 103).

5. Most students will probably disagree with Deb's evaluation for it has not worked itself out at all. The boy has been emotionally deprived of the love of one person and Deb has been deprived of giving her love. Perhaps more important to the boy as he listens to his stepmother's explanations is the fact that the decisions about the family relationships were made by others. "Above and about me, over my head, saving me the risk and the opportunity of my own volition" (page 103).

6. Although the boy had never known exactly what it was he had been missing, he now realizes he has missed having a mother. Supposedly he had two mothers, but both had abdicated the role, leaving the boy with simply two women. Finally realizing all of this, the boy blames Deb for she is the one he really would have liked to see fulfill the maternal role. It is Deb he has loved and admired. Ironically enough, she is the one who innately wanted to be his mother but who felt it was

for his benefit that she do nothing to destroy the image and role of his real mother.

Additional Questions

1. Explain the relevance to the story of the boy's feeling that Deb "had entered, irrevocably, the atavistic tensions of that cunning battle for love and supremacy that exist between children and parents sometimes even beyond the grave, when one protagonist is dead and mourned, and lives on in the fierce dissatisfaction of the other's memory" (page 96).

    It is at this point that the boy realizes that Deb has become an integral part of his existence. She is now a part of the battle for the love and attention that exists between the parents and the child. The boy will proceed to "use" Deb and his mother to win this "cunning battle for love and supremacy."

2. In what sense might it be truly said that the boy had two mothers and yet no mother?

    The boy had a natural mother and a stepmother. Both women were alive and a part of his daily life, yet neither woman fulfilled the role of mother. Each held a part of herself back from the boy, leaving him deprived of the maternalism he needed and craved.

3. Explain the significance of the title to the story as a whole.

    The story is not titled "My Two Mothers" for neither of these women fulfilled the role of mother in the boy's life. Instead a more impersonal, less emotional reference to "My First Two Women" is made. They are merely women, not unlike other women who will follow in his life.

Composition

Adjusting to Deb's presence, the boy suffers from undefined guilt feelings of disloyalty. "Disloyalty—to what? Guilty—of what?" he wonders. How would you answer the questions that trouble him?

A White Heron / p. 106
Sarah Orne Jewett (1849–1909)

The conflict between loyalty to the natural world and the emerging needs of a woman's heart is not settled without pain. Sarah Orne Jewett brings a sense of quiet compassion to this dilemma faced by a young "woods-girl."

Insight

1. Students will probably point out that Sylvia is a shy, lonely girl, happiest spending her time with nature rather than with people. She cheerfully exchanged her life in a congested manufacturing town for life on

the farm with Mrs. Tilley. "Sylvia whispered that this was a beautiful place to live in, and she never should wish to go home" (page 107). Hers was truly "an existence heart to heart with nature and the dumb life of the forest!" (page 111).

2. A shy person by nature, Sylvia is a lonely child. The stranger, even though he kills her companions from nature, has awakened in her a feeling of love. "She had never seen anybody so charming and delightful; her woman's heart, asleep in the child, was vaguely thrilled by a dream of love" (page 110).

3. Sylvia would very much like to please the stranger. "He is so well worth making happy, and he waits to hear the story she can tell" (page 113). At the same time, her own loneliness pushes her to share her secret of the heron. For then the two would be friends and after all, this is the first time that "the great world . . . puts out a hand to her," (page 113) inviting her to join. But upon reaching the top of the tree, she realizes how small the world is below her. She sees the heron as he cries to his mate and "plumes his feathers for the new day!" (page 113), and she sees the ocean for the first time. Her perspective is now from above, looking down to where she had been standing for a year. Her outlook is broadened.

4. Students will probably point out that although lonely and shy, Sylvia is neither cruel nor alone for she does have the natural world around her that has already given her great comfort. For her to destroy even a small part of this world would be for her to destroy her own love and comfort. Some students will feel that her attitude never really changed, for she never actually decided to give up the bird. Other students will feel that her loneliness was the cause of her desire to tell the stranger, but because she always had the companionship of the natural world, she would never be lonely enough to desert her friends in nature.

5. Sylvia's conflict is an internal one between her desire to please this stranger who has awakened "the woman's heart, asleep in the child" (page 110) and her own sense of being one with the natural world in which she lives. It is an expensive or "dear loyalty" for she chooses not to follow and love the stranger, but to remain a "woods-girl."

Additional Questions

1. Why do you suppose Sylvia initially refers to the stranger in the woods as "the enemy"? In what sense does he finally turn out to be her enemy?

    Answers will vary. Some students may suggest that the stranger has interrupted Sylvia in her pleasure of the woods. She had just been feeling "as if she were a part of the gray shadows and the moving leaves" (page 107). Suddenly this stranger interrupts her reveries and returns this shy "woods-girl" to the real world of people. Other students may point to the conclusion of the story as proof that the stranger is indeed, an enemy. Conniving to gain Sylvia's help in locating the heron, he becomes an enemy to the natural world and to Sylvia's world. Even so, Sylvia will eventually forget "her sorrow at the sharp report of his gun and the piteous sight of thrushes and sparrows dropping silent to the ground . . ." (page 114).

2. Describe the stranger's attitude and behavior toward Sylvia. Do you think he is being sincere with her, or is he merely kind to her in hopes that she can lead him to the heron? Explain.

   Some students will probably feel the stranger is insincere in his relationship with Sylvia. These students will point to his gift of a jack-knife as a bribe and his promise of ten dollars for the heron as a low inducement to a poor child. Other students, however, will suggest that these are not bribes at all, but gifts from a "friendly lad, who proved to be most kind and sympathetic" (page 110). No matter what his motivation may be, the young man is gallant and charming toward Sylvia, and her heart goes out to him.

Composition

Describe a situation from your own experience in which you were torn by conflicting loyalties. Which loyalty did you select at the time? In retrospect do you still think you made the right decision?

Effort at Speech Between Two People / p. 115
Muriel Rukeyser (born 1913)

Loneliness, desperation, and even a sense of humiliation surface as two people grope toward understanding themselves and each other. Rukeyser describes their effort at communication in this poignant poem.

Insight

1. Both people are lonely, seeking someone with whom they can share their lives. The first person is preoccupied with telling the woman stories from his or her past — when he or she was three, nine, fourteen. And the woman is as preoccupied with her personal tale of a former love. As the poem ends, both speakers are reaching out, groping for one another. "If we could touch one another,/if these our separate entities could come to grips" (lines 31–32). But their hands do not touch, their lives do not intertwine except for their shared sense of loneliness and isolation. It can only be hoped that their very loneliness will ultimately bring them together and then they will, as the first person says, "link the minutes of my days close, somehow, to your days" (line 16).

2. The mood of the poem is one of tender intimacy and longing. These two people are making a great effort to satisfy their longings and each speaks intimately of the past. Their tender yearnings for

communication, "Speak to me. Take my hand. What are you now?" (line 11) go all but unheeded as both people remain preoccupied with their own thoughts.

Composition

Write two descriptive paragraphs on how you envision the two people in the poem.

Her First Ball / p. 117
Katherine Mansfield (1888–1923)

Attending her first ball, a young girl is initiated into the actual joys and the potential sorrows of the adult world. This story by the English writer Katherine Mansfield captures the anticipation, the excitement, and the disillusion of that glamorous evening.

Insight

1. Leila's initial mood is one of excitement and anticipation. In the cab, "perhaps her first real partner," (page 117) she can hardly contain her pleasure as she speeds toward the ball. "Oh, dear, how hard it was to be indifferent like the others!" (page 117) she laments. But after reaching the ball, nervousness overtakes her, and she experiences the anxiety of rejection as she awaits her first partner. Her joy soon returns, and she dances blithely and eagerly until her dance with the fat man. Now her mood changes. "Leila gave a light little laugh, but she did not feel like laughing" (page 121). After this dance, she is no longer the radiant young girl but now a disillusioned, sad young woman. She had been forced to question whether her first ball was "only the beginning of her last ball after all?" (page 121). Her short-lived despair, however, is soon suppressed, and Leila concludes the ball almost as radiant and joyful as she began it.
2. The fat man has "been doing this kind of thing for the last thirty years" (page 121). He has seen many young women come to the dances, and he knows that they will all age and most will turn out like the ones sitting on the stage, the chaperons for the young. He does not mean to be cruel in his remarks, only realistic. But to romantic Leila at her first ball, the remarks are the depth of cruelty for they break the spell, and she is forced to face a reality for which she is not prepared.
3. Many students may feel this first ball might well have been the beginning of her last ball had she not been able to recapture the glow of her previous mood. If she had remained disillusioned and disappointed there might not have been another ball. After all ". . . Leila didn't want to dance any more. She wanted to be home, or sitting on the veranda listening to those baby owls" (page 122). She wanted to

pursue the interests of her childhood, not be swept unprepared into the adult world.

Additional Questions

1. What does Leila's need to tell her various partners that this is her first ball reveal about her? How is her revelation received?

    Leila's enthusiasm and naivete are both emphasized by her eagerness to explain herself to her partners. Her partners, however, are startled and embarrassed by such a revelation and don't quite know how to deal with it.

2. What is the significance of Leila's failure to recognize the fat man at the end of the story?

    Leila has blocked out the moment of impending adulthood and has restored herself to a world of illusion, a more childlike, romantic world.

3. Mansfield's descriptive powers are seen throughout the story. Cite descriptions that you found especially effective.

    Some students may point to images such as "Perhaps her first real partner was the cab," (page 117) or ". . . the bolster on which her hand rested felt like the sleeve of an unknown young man's dress suit" (page 117). Other students may well note the description of the women carrying the wraps or the effective description of the girls in the powder room as they prepare to meet their partners. Still other students may point to descriptions such as "a great quivering jet of gas lighted the ladies' room," (page 118) or the description of the fat man as "he wheezed faintly as he steered her past an awkward couple" (page 121).

Composition

Describe an event that you looked forward to with great anticipation. In what ways did the actual experience equal your feelings of anticipation? What changes in mood did you undergo in the course of the event?

In Summary

"Who am I?", that most intense of personal questions, has been asked through the centuries since first Socrates advised "Know thyself." The question rolls easily off the tongue; the answer is often paid for with pain.

Again and again the question appears in these selections—framed now by a nine-year-old girl in "The White Heron," now by an aging woman in "The Double Goer," now by a young boy in "My First Two Women." The search and the discovery bring pain and only tentative answers. The reflection in Nin's mirror has meaning but for today. Tomorrow the question must be asked again, the search begun anew.

"All is flux" wrote Heraclitus many years ago. So, too, with a human being. McGinley's girl with comic book grows into Levertov's seeking mind and becomes Laing's double goer. Only Samuel does not change.

Suggested Reading

*Giovanni, Nikki. *My House*. New York: Morrow, 1972.

Gordimer, Nadine. *Six Feet of the Country*. New York: Simon and Schuster, 1956.

*Jewett, Sarah Orne. *The Country of the Pointed Firs*. New York: Doubleday, 1954.

Levertov, Denise. *To Stay Alive*. New York: New Directions, 1971.

*Mansfield, Katherine. *The Garden Party and Other Stories*. London: Constable, 1922.

*McGinley, Phyllis. *The Love Letters of Phyllis McGinley*. New York: Viking Press, 1952.

Nin, Anaïs. *The Diary of Anaïs Nin*, volumes 1–5. New York: Harcourt Brace Jovanovich, 1974.

Paley, Grace. *Enormous Changes at the Last Minute*. New York: Farrar, Straus & Giroux, 1974.

*Petry, Ann. *Miss Muriel and Other Stories*. Boston: Houghton Mifflin, 1971.

Plath, Sylvia. *Ariel*. New York: Harper & Row, 1966.

Rukeyser, Muriel. *Waterlily Fire*. New York: Macmillan, 1962.

DRAMA

Trifles / p. 127
Susan Glaspell (1882–1948)

Does a woman worry only of "trifles" as some men apparently believe? Susan Glaspell, 1931 Pulitzer Prize winner for drama, examines the question in this play which is based upon an incident that occurred during her days of newspaper reporting.

Insight

1. Most students will agree that the Wrights are portrayed as quiet, reclusive country people. No one seems to know the couple well, and neighbors such as Mrs. Hale, have a rather low opinion of John's disposition. "But I don't think a place'd be any cheerfuler for John Wright being in it" (page 130). Mrs. Wright is remembered as having once been a lively and pretty young girl whose married years with John, however, have turned her into a shy, withdrawn woman. Those describing the Wrights appear to feel uncomfortable about them. Mrs. Hale expresses pity for them and sorrow that she never took time to visit. Although Hale was uncomfortable with John Wright, he felt friendly enough to inquire about a telephone line. Certainly everyone seems aware that the Wrights are an odd, unhappy couple.

2. Mrs. Hale has been a neighbor of Mrs. Wright and appears to be more sympathetic to her situation than is Mrs. Peters. Mrs. Hale expresses sorrow for not being more friendly and trying to bring some cheer into Mrs. Wright's life. "I could've come. I stayed away because it weren't cheerful . . ." (page 134). Mrs. Peters is a nervous woman, caught between her position as a sheriff's wife and her understanding of the darkness of another woman's life. She does not, however, have the strength of her convictions that Mrs. Hale reveals. The reader feels if the other woman weren't present, Mrs. Peters would be unable to conceal any information from the men. However, from the moment the dead canary is found, Mrs. Peters begins to reflect a real understanding of Mrs. Wright's position. "I know what stillness is" (page 136).

3. "Well, women are used to worrying over trifles," Hale comments complacently (page 129). And because they feel that is all women worry about, the men are blind to any evidence the women might uncover. Mrs. Peters is prone to support the men in their attitude for she has obviously been told for years that men have "got awful important things on their minds" (page 132). Mrs. Hale is less tolerant of this attitude and is willing to stand up for her own position.

4. The women find the dead canary and hide it, fully aware that this is the motive for John Wright's murder. The bird was the one note of

27

cheer in Mrs. Wright's bleak existence. "If there'd been years and years of nothing, then a bird to sing to you, it would be awful — still, after the bird was still" (page 136). Because all three women have experienced similar treatment from their husbands, there is a sense of understanding of Mrs. Wright's life. Even though the women are guilty of suppressing evidence, they feel justified in hiding it from the men who are utterly blind to them as thinking human beings. The rising bread, a clue representing the suddenness of the crime, and the nervous sewing, a clue to Mrs. Wright's state of mind, are also found by the women.

Additional Questions

1. Mrs. Peters is in the process of change throughout the play. What specific factors contribute toward her shifting attitude? How believable did you find her change?

    Most students will see Mrs. Peters initially as a rather nervous, mouse-like woman, parroting the words of her husband. She appears to become more aware of Mrs. Wright's position after the sewing is found, and finally she begins to take a strong position when the canary is found. "I know what stillness is," she says (page 136), and because she knows, she is able to have compassion and sympathy.

2. How does Mrs. Hale's innocent question "I wonder if she was goin' to quilt it or just knot it?" come to have ironic and symbolic significance in the course of the play?

    It is the two women who possess the evidence for the motive of the murder. And it is Mrs. Hale who says to the men, "We call it—knot it" (page 137). She speaks not just of the quilt, but also of the rope that was knotted around John Wright's neck.

3. "Oh I *wish* I'd come over here once in a while! That was a crime! That was a crime! Who's going to punish that?" cries Mrs. Hale. What does she mean by these words? What feelings of guilt do they suggest?

    Mrs. Hale feels a keen sense of responsibility for the other woman's unhappiness. "We all go through the same things—it's all just a different kind of the same thing," she explains to Mrs. Peters (page 136). Her own life with Hale, who believes "women are used to worrying over trifles" (page 129) has made her sympathetic to the frustrations of another woman. Further, she feels if she had visited and brought a little cheer to Mrs. Wright's depressing and isolating existence, the crime might have been averted.

Composition

1. Mrs. Hale remarks that "we live close together, and we live far apart." In an essay based on your own observations and experiences comment on the truth of this statement.

2. Write a newspaper report of the murder. Be objective in your reporting and do not include more evidence than is uncovered by the investiga-

tors. Then prepare a subsequent newspaper report of the outcome of the trial. Include the jury's verdict and a summary of the evidence presented in court.

A Raisin in the Sun / p. 138
Lorraine Hansberry (1930–1965)

Although her writing career was cut short by her untimely death at the age of thirty-four, Lorraine Hansberry contributed two unique plays to the American theater. *A Raisin in the Sun* was her first drama and reflects the author's keen sensitivity to the plight of the individual overwhelmed by powerful social forces.

Insight—Act I

1. *A Raisin in the Sun* is set in the Southside of Chicago sometime after World War II. The Younger's apartment is crowded with years of possessions accumulated by many people. The room exudes a tired air, an air of depressing heaviness. "Weariness has, in fact, won in this room" (page 139). One feels the people living in the room must also have a sense of weariness about them. Life has been hard on them; there doesn't appear to be in their lives more than that one ray of light "which fights its way through. . . ." The details of the setting provide additional information: that the Younger's are poor; that although poor, they, nevertheless, care about what they do have.

2. Most students will see that the members of the family have long been frustrated by the poverty and difficulty of their existence. Each personality has, therefore, developed within this context. Walter, for example, has been overpowered by a dominating although kindly mother which he sees as a parallel to a dominating society. Walter's sense of dignity has long been destroyed until now we see a thirty-five year old man full of self-hatred and contempt. "I been married eleven years and I got a boy who sleeps in the living room—and all I got to give him is stories about how rich white people live" (page 144). There is about him a sense of desperation as he appeals to the women to help him fulfill this dream. Beneatha is a stronger person than her brother. She has a sense of racial pride and a fighting spirit, if appearing at times, rather adolescent as she talks about horseback riding and guitar lessons. Mama is a tyrannical warm-hearted matriarch. One feels, however, that her tyrannical nature has been developed to protect her children not to harm them. Ruth is a rather sad, disappointed woman for whom "life has been little that she expected" (page 139). She obviously feels lost and defeated as she makes a down payment for an abortion.

3. Most students will probably see that many of the personal conflicts appear to revolve around the conflict over the inheritance money. Many other conflicts, however, come into focus in the first act. Arguing almost

incessantly, Ruth and Walter epitomize their disagreement when Walter says, "I got me a dream. His woman say: Eat your eggs" (page 144). He summarizes the conflict between them when he mumbles, "We one group of men tied to a race of women with small minds" (page 145). As Beneatha enters we see sibling conflict between her and Walter. This conflict again centers on a dream, this time Beneatha's dream to be a doctor. Later Beneatha will be in conflict with her mother over religion and George. She is also in conflict with her own identity in the scene with Asagai. Mama's conflict is primarily a generational one with her children. Their standards and behavior are not what she would wish.

4. Mama always wanted a garden for herself, she tells the children. Yet, it is for her children that she has the biggest dreams of happiness, security and even a "little old two-story somewhere, with a yard where Travis could play . . ." (page 149). Walter's dream is to own his own liquor business so he can escape his life of servility and escape as well a future of just "a big looming blank space—full of *nothing*" (page 164). Beneatha dreams of being a doctor, Ruth of a happy marriage and a sense of security. A lifetime of poverty, despair, and misunderstanding has kept the family from attaining their dreams.

Additional Questions

1. Of the characters introduced in Act I, Walter is the one whose outlook "about the world" is most clearly defined. How would you characterize his outlook? What lines are especially significant in revealing this outlook?

    Walter puts his entire faith in money. He sees money as the power that will save him from total degradation and provide him with the dignity he so desperately seeks. When Mama asks why he talks only about money, Walter replies "Because it is life, Mama" (page 164). And it would be, he believes, the source of new life for him. Without it, he is nothing, living in a "big, looming blank space." It is when he can give his son fifty cents for a taxi to school or can sit planning deals with his friend Bobo and Willy that Walter feels the big man. To Walter, ". . . don't *nothing* happen for you in this world 'less you pay *somebody* off" (page 144).

2. Beneatha is a young black girl frenetically searching for her identity. What effect does her family have upon this search? What effect does Asagai have?

    Many students will see that Mama and Asagai have almost opposite effects upon Beneatha in her search for her identity. Mama wants Beneatha to settle down and to find herself a rich husband. Beneatha reacts to this option with open contempt. She rejects her mother's views of God, of George Murchison and of security. At the same time, Beneatha cannot quite cope with Asagai's values either. He finds Beneatha too much of an assimilationist with her straightened hair and white middle class clothes. Yet Beneatha has been raised to strive for these and similar values (epitomized in her horseback riding and guitar lessons). Beneatha is, therefore, in an ambiguous position, still seeking her own identity.

3. While the play is basically a serious one, many elements of humor appear. What examples of humor can you find in the first act? What do these moments of humor contribute to the act as a whole?

The humor in Act I helps to relieve the moments of tension which build as a result of the continual conflicts among the characters. The humor further defines some of the characters. We see in Mama, for example, kindness, warmth, and sly humor as she attempts to please Beneatha in her greeting to Asagai. Ruth shows a similar warmth as she gently mocks Travis as he leaves the apartment unhappily.

Insight—Act II

1. Most students will see that Ruth and Walter seek different things from life. Walter wants wealth with the power and prestige that he assumes will accompany it, and he is willing to risk everything to reach his goal. Ruth, much more cautious, has simpler desires. She wants the stability of a happy home with a loving family, and she is not convinced that money can buy this for her. It is hard for Ruth and Walter to accept each other's positions. Walter sees Ruth as one more person who is rendering him powerless; Ruth feels Walter is ruining their marriage. There is a sign of hope, however, as the two briefly face their unhappiness and admit that things aren't good between them. "How we gets to the place where we scared to talk softness to each other" Walter asks (page 171).

2. Some students will sympathize with Walter and feel that Mama has butchered his dream. Because she always makes his decisions, Walter has yet to stand on his own feet. She has never allowed him to fulfill his own dreams as he has begged this time to do. Other students will feel less sympathy for Walter. They will see him as a thirty-five year old man who should be capable of more realistic dreams. Instead, his dreams are too grandiose, and he has allowed himself to be led by his mother for so long there is little chance he will know how to lead his own life. Others may sympathize with Mama's need to provide strength in a family situation where no male strength exists.

3. As Mama said earlier in the act, "I—I just seen my family falling apart today . . . just falling to pieces in front of my eyes . . ." (page 174). Before she gives Walter the money, she has seen him fall apart even more. To Mama the money is not worth the agony and misery Walter is suffering. "There ain't nothing worth holding on to, money, dreams, nothing else—if it means—if it means it's going to destroy my boy" (page 178). Walter is amazed that his mother would trust him with the money. She offers him the position of "head of the family," but

Walter, with his own dream foremost in his mind, is unable to meet the responsibility.

4. Lindner tells the Youngers that the neighborhood association will buy their home for more than they paid for it. The reason—to keep the Youngers from moving into their all-white neighborhood. The message is delivered in phrases of mutual respect and understanding. Beneatha appears to understand the message first, as she sarcastically responds to Lindner. Bitterness and contempt fill Walter as he slowly understands Lindner's purpose. Mama is more saddened, however, than her children. Perhaps she half expected some such action. The family feels pleased with their ability to stand firm against Lindner for they proudly and defiantly continue their packing. Their lightness stems from their seeing through Lindner's awkward attempt to con them into buying his "Brotherhood" package and their refusal to be intimidated by it.

Additional Questions

1. Living with his parents, his aunt, and his grandmother in a small apartment, Travis is naturally somewhat confused about the adults in his life. How has he learned to adjust and to cope with the somewhat disorganized and discordant household in which he finds himself?

   Travis has learned to play one adult off against another. When his mother does not give him what he wants, he turns to his father or his grandmother. Almost always someone is willing to side with him. Because his grandmother is most concerned with the generational ties, she appears to be the "softest touch" for Travis.

2. Two of the three scenes in Act II find George Murchison in the Younger household. How would you describe George's outlook on life? What feelings do you have toward him? What role does he appear to play in the drama?

   George is a pragmatist. "You read books—to learn facts—to get grades—to pass the course—to get a degree. That's all—it has nothing to do with thoughts," he explains to Beneatha (page 176). George has no patience with Beneatha's search for her identity. He wants her to be like him, or what she considers an assimilationist. Certainly he is the opposite type of character from Asagai as well as from Walter. He acts as a foil to Beneatha and to Walter as both search for their identities.

3. What differences between Mama and Walter are revealed by the manner in which they receive Bobo's news?

   Mama displays the strength and pride of years of living a difficult existence. Her immediate anger is replaced by deep sadness and a call to God for the strength to surmount this great disappointment. Walter, sobbing over his personal misfortune, turns into a screaming child not able to recognize the misery he has brought to the family, although he can see that the lost money "is made out of my father's flesh" (page 189).

Insight—Act III

1. The bitterness of lost dreams has overwhelmed Beneatha as the act opens. Nothing matters to her now; she sees no reason to care anymore for caring is too far from truth. Yet, as Asagai points out, the struggle toward truth is vital, and without this continuous struggle, we would be nothing. He accuses Beneatha of looking for an easy out by accepting her brother's childish mistake. " . . . You are grateful to him. So that now you can give up the ailing human race on account of it" (page 193).

2. Most students will feel that when Mama first appears in Act III she is a lost, beaten woman. Walter has destroyed her dreams of a lifetime as he has destroyed her faith in him. Mama tries to explain that her dreams were too grandiose anyway. "Just aimed too high all the time—," she reflects (page 196). Walter, however, offers a solution: sell out to Lindner. Even this course does not raise Mama to the heights of anger that it would have earlier. Although she makes it clear she is against selling out ("We ain't never been that dead inside" page 198) she also knows sadly that Walter is capable of such a deed. Mama appears to have lost her spirit, her potential for anger. She is left an old, disappointed woman. Only when Walter haltingly changes his position with Lindner does Mama gain strength and come alive again. Ironically it was Mama's voice that prodded Walter to change as she insisted that Travis stay and Walter show him "where our five generations come to" (page 198).

3. After these words, Walter turns around and shows that he will not just accept the world that was "give to me this way." Instead he will take a positive step toward changing that world by moving into an all-white neighborhood. He does want to be a man even before he says, "I tell you I am a *man*" (page 198), although unable to act like one. Only when faced with explaining to his own son the reason for his actions, can Walter act like a man and turn down Lindner's money. Beneatha then pays him the ultimate compliment, "That's what the man said" (page 201).

4. The plant represents Mama's stubborn struggle for survival. It is a symbol of her strength and endurance, of her refusal to give up hope. Both the plant and Mama have had to endure a hostile environment; both are a little worn by the struggle, but both have survived and will continue to survive.

Additional Questions

1. What reaction do you have to Asagai as he expounds his views about Africa and independence? Do you find him, for example, heroic?

self-centered? poetic? unrealistic? idealistic? What does he mean when he says to Beneatha, "They who might kill me even . . . actually replenish me"?

Many students will see Asagai as an heroic figure. They will see that he is meant to symbolize the self-confident, dignified man who has found his identity without destroying his roots and culture. He is a man aware of the possibility of his own destiny and aware that what he may become could soon be anachronistic for his nation and people. Thus, even if killed by his own brothers, his destiny would be fulfilled as his nation moves forward.

2. While Walter has clearly undergone a considerable change in outlook, note that at the end of the play he is advising Beneatha to marry George Murchison. How do you account for this piece of advice? Do you think Beneatha will eventually follow it? Explain.

Walter comes into his manhood by the play's end. He is able to put his personal dream aside and to see the heritage that five generations have left him. Feeling a man, he now wants to assume the responsibility of the family. Thus, he gives what could be considered practical advice to Beneatha. Beneatha may not marry George Murchison for whom she shows such contempt, but then she probably will not marry Asagai either for he and his country represent to her a part of the past, not a sign of the future.

Insight—The Play As a Whole

1. All of these things happen to the dreams. Although Beneatha's dream is deferred, one feels she will someday attain it. In the past, Walter's dream "festered like a sore" until the day it exploded. All that remained was the memory of that dream, a dream that was now "like a raisin in the sun." Of all the dreams in the play, Mama's finally comes to fruition. She has her house with a yard and most of all she has seen her children grow up. "He finally come into his manhood today, didn't he?" she says of Walter (page 202).

2. Most students will agree with the stated characterization. As a social protest drama, *A Raisin in the Sun* protests the plight of Negroes caught in the economic and social situation which strips them of their dignity and their sense of self. They are left to strive for the white man's values in the white man's world. Human drama is not to be overlooked for the play also has a strong human appeal and realistic characters. Their conflicts are all too understandable; their emotions, all too human. As Hansberry said of the play, it is "about honest-to-God, believable many-sided people who happen to be Negroes."

3. Most students will agree that Walter, Mama, Beneatha and Ruth seem very real. Their emotions and behavior are understandable in human terms. Asagai and George are presented in much more symbolic terms.

Asagai represents the self-confident, knowledgeable African who has faith in the destiny of his people and nation. George is symbolic of the assimilationist who will, no doubt, be successful in the society he chooses to enter.

4. Many students will feel Hansberry was speaking of the role our ambitions and dreams play in our lives. As Mama said, "Sometimes you just got to know when to give up some things . . . and hold on to what you got" (page 197). This point of realization may come slowly, but when it does come, one has reached a plateau of one's existence. In Walter's case, for example, he reached his manhood when he realized he had to give up one dream in order to hold on to another dream.

Additional Questions

1. In most plays the main characters are dynamic, that is they undergo significant changes in the course of the drama. Static characters, those that do not change, often tend to appear "wooden" to us. Which characters in this play seemed to you dynamic? Which static?

   Walter, Mama, and Beneatha are much more dynamic than the other characters. These three characters undergo turmoil and conflict, and emerge at the end of the play somewhat different people. George, Asagai and Ruth are much less dynamic characters whose positions do not change significantly during the course of the play. Instead these characters serve to contrast or clarify the ideas of the other characters.

2. The subplot of a play is a secondary or minor story which parallels the main story. What are the subplots in *A Raisin in the Sun?* How closely interwoven with the main plot do they appear to be?

   Beneatha's relationships with Asagai and George are one example of a subplot. Yet they are also vital to the main plot because they focus upon Beneatha's identity which will ultimately be seen in relationship to her dreams of being a doctor. Another example of a subplot is the relationship between Ruth and Walter. Their marriage is examined and in so doing, one is aware of the turmoil and conflicts within their characters. Thus, again, this subplot contributes to the reader's understanding of the characters involved in the main plot.

Composition

Write an essay in which you express your own ideas about one of the following quotations from the play. You may discuss the quotation in terms of either the play itself, your own observations, or your own experience.

1. "Once upon a time freedom used to be life—now it's money."
2. "You read books to learn facts—to get grades—to pass the course—to get a degree. That's all—it has nothing to do with thoughts."
3. "Sometimes you just got to know when to give up some things . . . and hold on to what you got."

4. "There ain't no causes—there ain't nothing but taking in this world, and he who takes most is the smartest—and it don't make a damn bit of difference *how*."

In Summary

These questions in the textbook deal not only with the two plays represented here but also with the more encompassing elements of all drama—dialogue, plot, characters, theme. Students should realize that these elements are common to all drama and are the playwright's means of accomplishing his or her purpose. Students often need to be reminded that plays are written primarily to be presented on the stage. Thus, the reading of a play is only the beginning of understanding it. The play should be visualized in terms of scenery, costumes, and vocal expression for it must be made to come alive before an audience's eyes.

Suggested Reading

If the collected works listed are not available, please check your own library listings as many of these plays are available in a variety of collected works.

Delaney, Shelagh. *A Taste of Honey* from *The New British Drama*, ed. Henry Popkin. New York: Grove Press, 1962.

*Glaspell, Susan. *Plays*. New York: Dodd Mead, 1948.

*Goodrich, Frances. *Diary of Anne Frank*. New York: Random House.

*Gregory, Lady Isabella. "Spreading the News" from *Twenty-Four Favorite One-Act Plays*, ed. Bennett Cerf. New York: Doubleday, 1958.

Hansberry, Lorraine. *The Sign in Sidney Brustein's Window*. New York: Random House, 1965.

———. *To Be Young, Gifted and Black: A Portrait of Lorraine Hansberry in Her Own Words*. Englewood Cliffs, N.J.: Prentice-Hall.

Hellman, Lillian. *Collected Plays*. Boston: Little Brown, 1972.

*Kerr, Jean. *Please Don't Eat the Daisies*. New York: Doubleday, 1971.

Luce, Clare Boothe. *The Women* from *The Best Plays of 1936–37*, ed. Burns Mantel. New York: Dodd Mead, 1937.

*McCullers, Carson. *A Member of the Wedding* from *Best American Plays: Third Series 1945–51*, ed. John Gassner. New York: Crown, 1952.

Millay, Edna St. Vincent. "Aria da Capa" from *Twenty-Five Best Plays of the Modern Theatre: Early Series*, ed. John Gassner. New York: Crown, 1949.

In a Role

Natural Law / p. 209
Babette Deutsch (1895–1974)

An Ancient Gesture / p. 210
Edna St. Vincent Millay (1892–1950)

What is woman's role? Why is it so often one of waiting, of loneliness? To this incessant plight these two American poets raise their voices in protest.

Insight

1. Many students will agree that in both poems the subject of loneliness is foremost. The speaker in "Natural Law" asks whether or not a woman can relieve the "whole weight of love" (line 10) as she sits "in the deep night, alone" (line 6). The speaker in "An Ancient Gesture" is concerned with the wiping of her tears, a gesture caused by her aloneness. Further, she thinks of ancient Penelope and of Ulysses and how they used their tears. Penelope, like the speaker in the poem, wiped her eyes for authentic reasons.

2. Most students may well feel the Millay poem is more bitter than the Deutsch poem. In "An Ancient Gesture" the speaker attempts to rationalize her own tears. She cried, but then so did Penelope, and for good reason, too! The words are tight; the tone is bitter. A woman has reason to cry. Sometimes "there is simply nothing else to do" (line 9). The speaker in "Natural Law" has a questioning attitude toward her situation. Yes, she is lonely, but is there a law of nature that dictates her feelings as easily as Newton explains his natural law? The implied answer to this question is one of resignation. There is not a natural law, but the situation is so much hers as to be almost inescapable.

Additional Question

How do the titles of each of these poems contribute to their meaning? How effective do you consider each title?

Students may point out the timeless quality suggested in each poem. The "gesture" is an ancient one, unchanging and ever-present through the ages. The "law," although not written, seems a natural one, determined by nature and unchangeable. Most students will feel the titles are particularly effective for they indicate a situation not unique to modern woman.

I Stand Here Ironing / p. 211
Tillie Olsen (born 1913)

Almost certainly every mother reflects upon her child's dependent years with a sense of fulfillment or of frustration, with a feeling of sorrow or of joy.

37

But even in the best of situations, how does a mother look back on those years without becoming engulfed "with what should have been and what cannot be helped"? The mother's situation, in this compassionate story by Tillie Olsen, has been far from the best; her sense of frustration, great; her feeling of guilt, deep.

Insight

1. Most students will probably feel that Emily has needed help for nineteen years and may well never receive the specific help she needs. Her mother now sees clearly what was needed: smiles, "the face of joy, and not of care or tightness or worry," (page 212) years of "proud love" not "anxious love," a mother's daily care and companionship.

2. Although the mother loves her daughter deeply, she admits she has no "key" to her daughter. "There is all that life that has happened outside of me, beyond me," (page 211) she says of Emily's nineteen years. She does feel guilty that she was not able to provide for Emily as she did for the other children, but all the while, she is aware that the circumstances of life itself were against them. "We were poor and could not afford for her the soil of easy growth ... My wisdom came too late" (page 217) she says of those early years. At the same time, however, she faces the burden of her guilt as she recognizes that Emily "has much in her and probably nothing will come of it" (page 217) as a result of the emotional deprivation of her childhood.

3. Many students will probably feel that Emily's mother has adjusted herself to a difficult life, one requiring her constant attention to the details of daily existence. She has never had time in the past to "total" up the years, and even now constant interruptions keep her from gathering the past together for evaluation. While her own intense personality may be a factor in this difficulty, poverty, war, and her personal situation have contributed to her inability to take the time "to sift, to weigh."

4. The mother knows that if she does succeed in evaluating Emily's past, she can only be caught up in greater feelings of guilt and self-recrimination. The antecedents to Emily's problems are, after all, in the past; little purpose would be served in becoming engulfed in them now. Despite this philosophical attitude, she does become engulfed as she stands there ironing and dredging up the past until she concludes, "Let her be."

5. Susan is everything Emily isn't but wishes she could be. She was brought up under more secure and happy circumstances (her mother had learned to show "the face of joy"), and life was made easier for her. Emily's resentment of Susan surely began as early as Susan's birth when Emily, suffering with the measles, had to be isolated from her mother and new sister. Soon thereafter, Emily was sent to a convalescent home, no doubt feeling "replaced" by the new baby. Years of

"corroding resentment" must have followed as she was asked to fulfill the role of mother: finding shoes, combing hair, and packing lunches for the smaller children while their mother had to be off earning a living.

6. "In a couple of years when we'll all be atom-dead they won't matter a bit," (page 217) Emily says of her mid-term exams. Her pessimistic, defeatist attitude particularly disturbs her mother for Emily's mother never quit, never looked at life as a temporary state where one did not need to make an effort. Instead, through the depression, the war, a broken marriage, she fought to survive, always believing in a better tomorrow, never giving in to hopelessness.

Additional Questions

1. Note that Emily is nineteen, the same age as her mother when Emily was born. What possible significance might this fact have on the story? Might the similarity in age imply some hope for Emily's eventual fate?

   Emily's mother shouldered heavy responsibility at the age of nineteen. As she admits, she was not necessarily successful, but she did survive; her child is now almost grown up and even if "... all that is in her will not bloom ... in how many does it?" Emily's mother did what she felt she had to do, and her life, after all, can hardly be considered a complete failure. Perhaps Emily, too, will survive, will find yet "enough left to live by."

2. To what extent is the time of the story and the events that take place a factor in the formation of Emily's character?

   As the mother states, Emily "is a child of her age, of depression, of war, of fear" (page 217). Had the early years been easier economically so the family did not have to live in poverty, had the depression not absented one father and the war another, Emily would, no doubt, have been a different person. She might have smiled easily, been at ease with others, had fewer psychological problems to preoccupy her young life.

3. How would you explain the mother's comment, "My wisdom came too late"? To what wisdom do you think she is referring? How accurate do you feel this evaluation is? Explain.

   The mother is referring to her understanding of those factors that have created the person Emily is today. Certainly, she sees her daughter from a perspective of time, yet this perspective comes too late to change the years of deprivation Emily suffered.

Composition

Explain in your own words the meaning and significance of the final paragraph of the story. Note whether you feel the ideas expressed are optimistic or pessimistic and support your position.

Little Girl, My String Bean, My Lovely Woman / p. 219
Anne Sexton (1928–1974)

Amusing Our Daughters / p. 223
Carolyn Kizer (born 1925)

Morning Song / p. 225
Sylvia Plath (1932–1963)

Sleep, Darling / p. 226
Sappho (600 B.C.)

Of these four poets, only Carolyn Kizer is still alive. Plath and Sexton, the other two contemporary poets, committed suicide at the height of their careers. Sappho, the Greek poet who wrote in the seventh century B.C., joins the three contemporary writers in viewing a child from a mother's perspective.

Insight

1. Although the speaker in Sylvia Plath's "Morning Song" appears to display a feeling of detachment toward her child as she says in lines 6–7, "I'm no more your mother than the cloud that distils a mirror . . ." the depth of her feeling soon becomes evident. Admitting that she wakes up just to listen for the child's cry, the speaker's tenderness and devotion become clear as we see her after that first cry stumbling out of bed "cow-heavy and floral in my Victorian nightgown." The speaker in Anne Sexton's poem "Little Girl, My String Bean, My Lovely Woman" shows devotion and love for her daughter quite openly. The mother feels both joy and apprehension as she watches her daughter grow into a woman. The poem is a plea to the speaker's daughter—a plea to revel in her approaching adulthood, to be sure of herself. The speaker in Sappho's poem takes a much more adoring attitude toward her child. From these few lines one can almost envision a tiny daughter who means more than anything else in the world to her parent. Finally, Carolyn Kizer's poem, "Amusing Our Daughters," displays a much more matter-of-fact attitude toward not only the speaker's daughter, but also toward life and death themselves. There is in the poem a feeling of maternal tenderness mixed with a sense of worldly understanding. Even though a daughter has died since a previous visit, this visit can continue with little effort because of the recognition of the temporal quality of life. "In time we will lose all our daughters, you and I" (line 22). Most students will probably agree that either the Sexton poem or the Sappho poem is more explicit in its display of love for the child. The Kizer poem, most students will probably agree, exhibits a greater sense of detachment than the other poems.
2. Most students will probably agree that the Sexton poem reveals a

joyous mood. As the speaker's daughter approaches adulthood, the speaker is reminded of her own early years and of her daughter's previous years. But mostly she thinks of the years yet to come and of the experiences yet to be. "I say hello to such . . . goings-on!" (lines 77–82). Students will point to the Sappho verse as displaying serenity. In these few lines the poet simply and quietly reveals the depth of her love and adoration for her child.

Additional Questions

1. Which poet deals most strongly in sense impressions? Which is least concerned with them? What images seem to you most effective in these poems? What emotions are conveyed as a result of these images?

   Most students will probably feel that the Plath poem is strongest in imagery. The entire poem is built upon the image of approaching dawn. Images of pastel colors such as the pink roses, floral gown, and whitened stars, create a feeling of lightness and well-being. Images of sound such as the slap of the midwife, the bald cry, echoing voices bring movement and life to the poem and stand in contrast to those quiet, light images of color. Most students will probably feel the Kizer poem reveals the least emphasis on imagery. Here the poet speaks matter-of-factly embroidering little upon actual events or emotions. This style, however, accentuates her entire attitude and purpose: "But even death becomes part of our ease" (line 15).

2. In which poem is the setting most important? Which details helped to clarify the time and place of the poem? Choose some particularly clear passages that establish the setting.

   Students may point to Plath's poem as the one in which setting is most important. All the details of the day contribute to making this truly a morning song. Lines 15–16 clarify the time of the poem, speaking of the disappearance of the night's stars, "The window square whitens and swallows its dull stars." Some students may point to the Sexton poem as an example of the importance of setting. In this poem a setting of time is emphasized—the approaching twelfth year of the speaker's daughter.

Everything That Rises Must Converge / p. 227
Flannery O'Connor (1925–1964)

A Southern author by birth and by tradition, O'Connor said of her writing, "My people could come from anywhere, but naturally, since I know the South, they speak with a Southern accent." The accent may be Southern, but the themes of her stories have no regional boundaries. In this story, for example, O'Connor explores the depth of scorn a son has for his mother and the overwhelming sense of guilt that results.

Insight

1. Her behavior on the bus is that of an innocent, wide-eyed child, one who has experienced little of the real world and remains untouched by shifting social patterns. She is completely unaware that her unkind remarks and actions are inappropriate. Her prejudiced comments about the Negro sound as if they come from a person living in another era. She sees nothing wrong with trying to give the child money, rather "the gesture would be as natural to her as breathing" (page 238).

2. Most students will see Julian as a complex person, indeed. He imagines himself as being in the vanguard of the social movement, yet, in reality, his deeds are done more for spite of his mother than for altruistic reasons. He is educated and sensitive to some things, yet to others, such as his mother, he displays only scorn and intolerance. While he professes sensitivity to other human beings, he is cruel to his mother.

3. The relationship between Julian and his mother is a close and intricate one. Although held by maternal bonds, Julian is tormented by his mother's obsolete values that conflict with his view of the new social order. He sees himself as emotionally free from his mother, but in truth, he is economically dependent upon her as well as emotionally dependent. The two make sacrifices for one another and in doing so become martyrs, proud of their struggles. Both mother and son are alienated not only from one another but alienated as well from the society in which they live. Julian believes "that with a few exceptions there was no one worth knowing within a radius of three hundred miles."

4. If his mother were a miserable human being, Julian feels he would be justified in hating her. As it is, her outworn gentility and graciousness leave her defenseless. Thus his spiteful attacks upon her fail to provide the satisfaction Julian seeks.

5. Julian unsuccessfully attempts to teach his mother "that the old world is gone. The old manners are obsolete and your graciousness is not worth a damn . . . You aren't who you think you are" (page 240).

6. Julian's mother is content for the Negroes to rise, "yes, but on their own side of the fence" (page 229). But as O'Connor states in the title and suggests in the story, as the Negroes rise, they will eventually meet and come together with the white race on one side of the fence. The races will not stay apart, as Julian's mother wishes. " 'You needn't act as if the world had come to an end,' Julian said, 'because it hasn't. From now on you've got to live in a new world and face a few realities for a change' " (page 240). The old world Julian's mother sought to preserve must give way to new rising social forces.

Additional Questions

1. Reread the opening paragraph of the story. Note the great amount of information O'Connor has provided in this one paragraph. What

specific things do you learn about Julian and about his mother? What things are implied about the two people?

Specifically, the reader learns that Julian's mother is attending a downtown reducing class because she suffers from high blood pressure. Because she is afraid to ride buses now that they are integrated, Julian escorts his mother to the weekly class. The paragraph implies that Julian's mother is a prejudiced woman whose relationship with Julian is strained. It further implies that Julian is unhappy not only with his weekly duty, but also with his mother and her sense of sacrificing for him.

2. A good writer can take an insignificant item such as a hat and imbue it with a significance far beyond its actual meaning. Trace O'Connor's use of the hat in this story. What is its initial significance? What is its later significance?

The hat appears in the very beginning of the story as Julian's mother prepares to leave for the Y. It is a new hat, and she wears it as a sign of her graciousness and good taste. Julian, however, finds the hat pathetic and is depressed that the hat should be so important to his mother. On the bus, however, the hat appears on the head of a black woman who wears it as proudly as Julian's mother. "That was your black double," Julian says to his mother. "She can wear the same hat as you . . . What all this means . . . is that the old world is gone" (page 240).

3. The reality of the present is difficult for Julian's mother to accept. As a result she often appears to be living in the past. What examples can you find which show her behavior to be grounded in the past rather than the present?

Students may point to such items as the gloves and hat she wears to a Y reducing class as an example of Julian's mother's living in the past. Certainly her attitude toward blacks, her evaluation of the women in her class as "not our kind of people . . . but I can be gracious to anybody. I know who I am" (page 229) are the values important to those living in another era.

4. What is the significance of the decayed mansion? How do Julian and his mother feel about it? How would you explain Julian's feeling that "it was he, not she, who could have appreciated it?" Do you think he is correct? Explain.

The decayed mansion represents the old world with its pride in family and familial allegiance. It is symbolic of that past world which is forever lost to Julian's mother. Julian recognizes his mother's attachment to the mansion, but he is realistic enough to know that particular world is past. Because of his greater sensitivity toward beauty and graciousness, Julian feels he would appreciate the mansion more than his mother ever would. Most students will feel that Julian does appear to be the more sensitive of the two characters, and no doubt, he would be the one for whom the mansion would hold the greatest pleasure.

5. What "symbolic significance" does Julian attach to the incident with the black woman and her child on the bus?

Julian believes the incident should prove to his mother "that the old world is gone. The old manners are obsolete and your graciousness is not worth a damn" (page 240). As a matter of fact, her graciousness is no longer gracious. Instead it is insulting and reveals her prejudice. Julian is wrong, however, when he says that it would not kill her to face reality, to live in the world as it is today. It is precisely this—her physical contact with the real world—that does kill her.

6. Discuss the significance of the last sentence.

Julian has not appeared to feel much love or affection for his mother. Yet in this last sentence and in his frantic efforts to revive her, one can see his love mixed with his fear of being totally alone in the world. He will live in a "world of guilt and sorrow" for not having been more tolerant of the only human being who really cared for him.

Composition

1. "If you know who you are, you can go anywhere," exclaims Julian's mother (page 228). Discuss this quotation in terms of Julian and his mother. Do they know themselves? Cite specific references to support your opinion.

2. It is not unusual for a child to be in conflict with the manners and values of his or her parents. Describe one area of conflict that you have observed or experienced. How would you identify the source of the conflict? How would you have liked to see the conflict resolved?

A Woman Mourned By Daughters / p. 242
Adrienne Rich (born 1929)

Adrienne Rich examines in this poem the impact of a mother's death upon her daughters. As in all of her poetry, Rich speaks precisely and exactly with a tone of personal commitment.

Insight

1. The daughters' love for their dead mother is evident as they feel her presence fill the room. They are weighted down by the heaviness of death and by their love for this woman. The daughters know precisely what their mother would desire of them, and as the speaker says, they would never dare do anything "save exactly" as she would desire.

2. Students should point to line 9 "like a corpse pulled from the sea," lines 10–11 "And yet you were a leaf, a straw blown on the bed," and

lines 25–26 "seas of carpet, a forest of old plants to be watered." The overall effect achieved by the use of this imagery, some students will agree, is to convey a sense of life, of motion. Even though the mother is dead, her spirit is alive and overwhelms the daughters as they sit at the table mourning.

Additional Questions

1. Discuss the meaning of lines 22–24 beginning, "You breathe upon us now through solid assertions of yourself . . ."

   These lines exemplify the strength and power of the mother that remains even after her death. Her presence is all around the daughters in the form of household items, "plants to be watered" and even the mother's husband to be cared for.

2. What has been the daughters' relationship with their mother? What is ironic about their present situation?

   The daughters are now married women who sit in their dead mother's kitchen with "not a tear begun." For years they were fed and clothed by this woman who felt "nothing could be enough." Their love for her is evident as is their own sense of not having done enough for her. They "succeeded in ignoring" her—not a conscious gesture perhaps, but a gesture symbolic of their own growing independence. Now they mourn for their mother, a woman of such power and strength that even after her death they are aware of her presence and her "solid assertions." It is ironic that for so many years the mother prodded the daughters with food and took care of them, and now they are left to care for those "solid assertions" she has left behind.

The Little Bouilloux Girl / p. 243
Sidonie-Gabrielle Colette (1873–1954)

Colette, the prolific French author of novels and stories concerned with women's various roles in life, examines here the effect extraordinary beauty can have upon a woman's existence.

Insight

1. Most students will probably agree that it was not only the little Bouilloux girl's rare beauty that isolated her from other people, but her excessive vanity as well. Nana's pride in herself "as a beautiful creature would not let her turn her eyes . . . giggle like her companions" (page 245). It is Nana's arrogant pride that frustrates her dream for eventual happiness. Never will she be able to find "a stranger, a ravisher" (page 246) who could be equal to her own vain image of herself.

2. As a young, beautiful child, Nana was constantly admired and petted and praised. By the time she was thirteen, she had already acquired a haughty manner and was "always unkind, but full of laughter

provoking boldness in those who would have been content merely to love her" (page 245). After the visit by the Parisians, however, her arrogant friendliness evaporated; she became even more aloof as she awaited her stranger. "She was simply waiting, possessed by an arrogant faith, conscious of the debt owed by the hazard that had armed her too well" (page 246).

3. Students will probably point out that Nana appears almost ten years older than her thirty-eight years at the end of the story. There is now little evidence of the proud beauty that so enchanted everyone in earlier years. Instead, a woman whose face reveals bitterness and animosity continues to wait for her "ravisher." Nana Bouilloux has not lost faith in her now-faded beauty. She may never be found by her stranger, but she will continue to await him.

Additional Questions

1. What does the narrator's mother really mean when she speaks of "the complete uniform of a little Bouilloux girl"? How would you explain her comment, "It's just a matter of choice"?

   The narrator's mother describes to her daughter the pattern Nana's life will no doubt take. It is, she suggests, a pattern typical of young girls of Nana's type—vain girls spoiled by the attention given them. If one chooses to be this type of person and to become apprenticed at thirteen, then the chignon, the long skirts, the admirers, even the illegitimate child may all follow because such is the path or "the uniform of all little Bouilloux girls throughout the world, at thirteen—more's the pity" (page 244).

2. Explain the sadness and the truth of Colette's line, "And after that, nothing more ever happened to the little Bouilloux girl."

   Most students will probably feel the line clearly sums up the fruitless years Nana spends waiting for her "ravisher." The Parisians were worldly, traveled men whose admiration and praise for Nana simply exaggerated her own sense of worth. She saw herself as very special indeed; her stranger would have to be equally special. She would await him forever, but sadly, there would never be anyone to equal her vain opinion of herself.

Composition

Describe a person in whom you have noted some change in physical appearance since last you saw him or her. Explain your reaction to this change and attempt to evaluate the reason you reacted as you did.

A Tin Butterfly / p. 248
Mary McCarthy (born 1912)

A noted contemporary author of both fiction and non-fiction, Mary

McCarthy writes with a compelling clarity and an acerbic wit. In this selection she examines five years of her youth spent in the household of a misguided aunt and a sadistic uncle.

Insight

1. The early years with her parents are remembered almost glowingly by McCarthy, although she realistically admits that the children were spoiled by kind and indulgent parents. After these first happy years, the contrast with their later life with Myers must have been all the more devasting to the children.

2. Most students will probably feel a strong dislike for this fat, indolent man who took great pleasure in watching the children suffer. He beat them physically for the smallest misdeeds, but more significantly, he attempted to beat them psychologically as well. They were allowed no toys or diversions; he made candy for himself, but allowed them only to watch, never to share. "Such techniques, of course, are common in concentration camps and penal institutions," McCarthy states (page 261). His selfishness appears to be related to a sadistic nature that showed no signs of weakening. However, as McCarthy suggests, Myers did not ask for the task of rearing four children under the age of seven, nor did he ever feel comfortable with or equal to the McCarthy relatives. His own sense of inferiority no doubt fed his sadistic nature.

3. "... What I learned from this, in the main, was a policy of lying and concealment; for several years after we were finally liberated, I was a problem liar" (page 257). Probably her interest in books stemmed from rebelling against Myers' edict that the children could not read at home. The children, needing a fantasy world to which to escape, also made up stories of their own using the dictionary or school texts for inspiration. Finally, McCarthy attributes her dislike of the use of dialect in writing to being forced to listen to Uncle Myers' constant reading of the Uncle Remus tales.

4. Most students will probably point to McCarthy's statement that "my aunt was not a bad woman; she was only a believer in method" (page 258). Aunt Margaret's intentions were clear enough, "shape up those spoiled children." But if her nature was not unkind, her methods were crude and harsh. These methods were certainly encouraged by Myers as he prodded Margaret into even crueler ones. McCarthy gives her aunt credit for small kindnesses and attempts to judge her fairly. Obviously, her feelings are ambivalent toward this woman who worked hard to give four children what she, at least, considered best.

5. To find that Uncle Myers pinned the tin butterfly to the tablecloth himself is to have solid evidence of his deceitful, sadistic, and conniving nature. It is not that the reader was unaware of this before, but always in mind was the thought that McCarthy was telling the story. How

objective was she really being? The incident, coldly related, ends all doubt about Myers' true character.

Additional Questions

1. Describe the relationship between Myers and Margaret. Do the two appear to love each other? Which is the dominant partner in the marriage? Do you think theirs has been a successful marriage?

    Most students will no doubt agree that Margaret, deeply in love with Myers, becomes subservient to all his wishes. She acquiesces to his demands, feeds him special meals, beats the children if he so much as suggests it. Uncle Myers, although the dominant figure, was passive in his feelings for Margaret. He apparently did not dislike her, but "very likely it was his power over her that he loved and the power he had to make her punish us was perhaps her strongest appeal to him" (page 253).

2. Myers is described as "the perfect type of rootless municipalized man who finds his pleasures in the handouts of an industrial civilization" (page 253). What is meant by this description? In view of his pattern of behavior, how accurate a description of Myers does it appear to be? Cite specific examples to support your answers.

    Students may agree that this is, indeed, an accurate description. This passage portrays a man lacking all creativity, all originality. He is a product of a mechanized state, and he gains his pleasures from those civic activities in which he can simply observe, not participate or lead. Lacking inner resources, he is entertained by activities such as weighing himself on penny scales or taking streetcar rides.

3. To what extent, if any, does McCarthy's own attitude and behavior contribute to the tin butterfly incident? To what extent, if any, does Myers' obvious partiality toward Sheridan contribute?

    McCarthy took no pains to hide her feelings of malevolence toward her uncle. Often she assumed an attitude of superiority; other times, an attitude of aloofness. The small mind of her uncle must have been infuriated, until he finally was able to plan a revenge—hiding the tin butterfly. How appropriate that Myers should use as his weapon, something belonging to Sheridan, the blond, favored child.

4. What does McCarthy imply about her attitude toward both Myers and Grandpa Preston when she states, "Hence it was on a question of health that this good American's alarms finally alighted; the rest of what we poured out to him he either did not believe or feared to think of, lest he have to deal with the problem of evil"?

    McCarthy implies that Grandpa Preston, rather than wishing to confront the reality of possible evil inherent in the character of Myers, prefers to take action on a minor, almost unrelated complaint—the child's not wearing her glasses. Also clearly implied in this passage is

McCarthy's judgement of her Uncle Myers who makes the problem of evil a reality.

Composition

1. The events in "A Tin Butterfly" are described from the perspective of forty years. Analyze the tone and attitude McCarthy takes toward those early years. How do you suppose her point of view toward the events she describes has changed over the years?
2. Select a relative of your own and describe his or her physical appearance, personality, idiosyncracies. Be certain to choose language and examples that vividly portray this relative.

More of a Corpse Than a Woman / p. 270
Muriel Rukeyser (born 1913)

Seminary / p. 271
Constance Carrier (born 1908)

What danger does conformity pose to a woman's life? Might she become Rukeyser's "leaden woman" and never attempt to fulfill her true potential? Both Constance Carrier and Muriel Rukeyser protest strongly against such women and their conforming, wasted lives.

Insight

1. Both poems reflect an attitude of dismay and disgust with "academy girls" (line 2) and the "well-protected woman" (line 25) who happily exist molded into a particular pattern. In neither poem does anyone attempt to break the mold. Instead, everyone seems content to be "as much alike as peas or pearls"—those "dull girls with the educated minds and technical passions."
2. In both poems the women accept whatever role is handed to them. The seminary students "are not rebels, not at all" (line 19). They dress alike and become "group-blurred to any casual glance" (line 10). The only differences between the students in the Carrier poem and the women in the Rukeyser poem are their ages and their experiences. The older women are referred to as "expensive girls, the leaden friends" (line 8). They wander from school reunions to marriage-suppers, yet, like the students, these women are "well-protected" (line 25), living an existence prearranged for them.
3. Most students will probably agree that the women in both poems fail to recognize their conformity to a pattern of living characteristic of their respective social groups. In neither case is there any hint that someone might seek to break the pattern, to examine her own individual nature and to attempt to fulfill it. It is Rukeyser who protests the loudest

against such uniform women in lines 28–30: "When your women are ready and rich in their wish for the world,/destroy the leaden heart,/ we've a new race to start."

Additional Question

Note that the Rukeyser poem might well be read as a continuation of the Carrier poem. What patterns of behavior by the young women in "Seminary" appear to be repeated by the older women in "More of a Corpse Than a Woman"?

The young women walk together, wear a uniform as "their defense against a too-large world" (lines 6–7), and recognize "their own elect" (line 21). The older women in the Rukeyser poem travel together, follow similar "technical passions" (line 10), even fall into a pattern of similar love affairs. They live a pattern established in their youth, a pattern of conformity that continues throughout their adult lives.

A Domestic Dilemma / p. 272
Carson McCullers (1917–1967)

In much of her writing, Carson McCullers concerned herself with the "immense complexity of love" and its effect upon those involved. In this story, Martin Meadows is faced with the responsibility of an alcoholic wife and two children. How does one cope with and overcome the sense of loneliness and frustration which must result?

Insight

1. Martin Meadows faces the domestic dilemma of whether to remain with his wife, who has become an alcoholic, or to leave her. Most students will point to the last line of the story as indicating that no matter how difficult life at home is, Meadows will probably not leave his wife.
2. Meadows blames the family's move from the South to New York, with all its attendant complications and changes, as the source of his wife's difficulties. She simply has not, he feels, made the adjustment to their new environment. Emily, who has family and friends in Alabama, has been unable to overcome the sense of loneliness created by the move and by a busy husband.
3. Students may cite the accident Emily had with the baby after the bath as the immediate source for Martin's anxiety for the children. Certainly, the general instability of his home situation would create further feelings of anxiety over the children's welfare. Other students will cite Martin's own thoughts on the quality of his love for his children. He admits to feeling a love that is "graver, touched with a strain of melancholy, a gentleness that was akin to pain" (page 279) for his daughter. Perhaps this feeling will be seen as a transference of his own love for his wife. Martin's feelings for his son are more casual, less grave. He is

able to call him nicknames and to joke with him about such things as the tooth tree, yet Martin appears to feel no less love for the boy than for the girl.

4. Many students will be immediately reminded of the last line regarding Martin's feeling of "immense complexity of love" for his wife. Contrasted with this is his intense antipathy when he thinks of what is happening to them as a family and to his own career. "He suffered a moment of rebellion against his fate; he hated his wife" (page 279).

Additional Questions

1. Note the parallels in the descriptions of Marianne and Emily asleep. What significance can you attach to these parallels?

Both descriptions convey a sense of quiet, a sense of innocence. The serenity of the sleeping daughter and the sleeping wife help to erase the tension and ugliness of the past hours. Martin is left with a feeling of love and a sense of protection. Because of these emotions, one is led to believe Martin will remain to care for his family.

2. How would you characterize the changes in Martin's mental outlook toward both life in general and his home in particular as a result of his wife's drinking?

Martin's anxiety about what he might find when he gets home has created a fear of going home, a dislike of home itself. "But in the last year nearness brought only a sense of tension and he did not anticipate the journey's end" (page 272). But it is not just his home which now leaves him with these feelings of anxiety. He is afraid people in the town and people in his office will begin to understand the situation and to pity him. He exaggerates the results of their finding out: "There was no hiding the truth—soon there would be gossip in the office and in the town; his wife was a dissolute woman. Dissolute. And he and his children bound to a future of degradation and slow ruin" (page 280).

3. Does Martin appear more concerned with his wife's problem or rather with the implications of that problem to his own reputation and life? Support your opinion with specific references from the story.

Many students may feel Martin spends little time trying to help his wife surmount her drinking problem. He has provided the children with someone to care for them, but he has sought no help for his wife nor does he seem particularly sympathetic to her difficulties. He has analyzed her problems from his point of view, but has taken no steps to delve into her point of view. He finds his life full of tensions and depression, yet he does not attack the problem. Instead, he makes excuses and attempts to avoid situations in which his wife might create a scene. Other students may feel that Martin is primarily concerned with his wife's difficulties, but caught up in the problems of daily existence, he does not have the time that is necessary to give to her.

4. What significance can you attach to the story of the tooth tree?

McCullers uses the story to portray the knowledge of the young boy who sees through the adult lie of the tooth tree. Martin asks, " 'Who does put it there?' 'Your parents,' Andy said. 'You!' " (page 279). Martin lies to his son about the small matter of the tooth, and he will lie about the larger problem of Emily's drinking. His desperation to hide the family problems, even from his own eyes, complicates Martin's attempt to cope.

Composition

All people at sometime or other have ambivalent feelings toward those they love. "The immense complexity of love itself" assures such feelings. Describe some person—parent, friend, teacher perhaps—toward whom you have ambivalent feelings. Make an attempt to analyze why you are beset by such strong contradictory feelings.

The Farmer's Bride / p. 283
Charlotte Mew (1869–1928)

The 5:32 / p. 284
Phyllis McGinley (born 1905)

To My Dear and Loving Husband / p. 285
Anne Bradstreet (1612?–1672)

Who can predict the interaction of individual personalities in a relationship? Why are some marriages blessed with elation, others with satisfaction, and still others with fear and loneliness? These three poems present three distinct views of the "complexity of love."

Insight

1. The speaker in the Bradstreet poem is most outspoken in her love for her husband. Theirs is obviously a warm, happy relationship in which they share a love prized "more than whole mines of gold" (line 5). The speaker in the McGinley poem is comfortable in her marriage. She will always remember her husband's return on the 5:32 as he comes toward her, "smiling, the evening paper under his arm, and his hat pushed back on his head" (lines 11–12). The farmer's bride, however, in the Mew poem, contrasts sharply with the other two women for the bride is miserable in her marriage, "afraid of love and me and all things human" (lines 4–5).

2. The farmer's bride has no relationship with her husband, no matter how longingly he may desire her. She is afraid and has hidden herself from him. The wife of the commuter in the McGinley poem plays the role of reliable help-mate. She is apparently so used to meeting the train that she does not stop to question the dailiness of the routine.

Every day the same routine, the same faces along the way, but it was the best hour "of all the hours I knew" (line 4) for it was the hour of her husband's return. The speaker in the Bradstreet poem plays the role of adoring wife ever so thankful that she has so loving a husband.

3. In the Bradstreet poem, the depth of the couple's love is emphasized by these thoughts of death. The wife wishes their love could last forever, even after death. In the McGinley poem, the act of picking up her husband and his return from a day's work, has been etched upon her memory. It has been such a significant part of their life together that if her world were torn in two, it would remain her single, most vivid impression. The fleeting thought of death makes each wife more loving, more grateful for what she has.

Additional Question

What are the different reactions to autumn in "The 5:32" and "The Farmer's Bride"? How do the different reactions indicate something about the two wives?

The reaction to autumn in "The 5:32" is one of serenity and satisfaction at the season's beauty. Autumn is a very real part of this woman's daily scene; it is now; it is to be appreciated. In the Mew poem, however, autumn serves merely as a precursor of the normally joyful Christmas season, a season which in this home forbodes sadness and loneliness with the bride fearfully separated from her husband.

Composition

During a lifetime all people fill roles of one kind or another. We are, for example, someone's child, another person's pupil, still another's friend. Describe one role in which you have found yourself. Discuss those aspects of the role that you found enjoyable and comfortable as well as those aspects you found difficult and uncomfortable.

The Yellow Wallpaper / p. 286
Charlotte Perkins Gilman (1860–1935)

Trapped in a world which credits her with neither intellect nor soul, the narrator of this chilling tale escapes in the only manner available to her. This remarkable, long-overlooked story by Charlotte Perkins Gilman, an early feminist, assumes added significance when viewed in the context of the present.

Insight

1. Most students will probably agree that John dominates his wife's life while she passively submits to his orders and demands. Initially she

acquiesces to this role for John "is very careful and loving, and hardly lets me stir without special direction" (page 287). He has already made her feel guilty for being the cause of their summer move, her guilt increasing whenever she attempts to rebel against one of his wishes. As the story progresses, the wife becomes angry with John's total blindness to what she is going through. She tries to explain her feelings to him, but as a doctor he sees from a scientific point of view that she is improving. So no reason for further discussion exists. The wife begins to spend her days deceiving her husband, hiding from him all suggestions of her true feelings. The wallpaper becomes an obsession toward which she directs her mind and emotions, locking John totally out of her existence.

2. The wife, trapped in the culture and mores of nineteenth century America, is aware of the hopelessness of her situation. The men in her life, the masters of her fate, say nothing is wrong other than "a slight hysterical tendency" (page 286). Their prescription of rest is not to be quarreled with for she sees herself as *only* a woman. She may want to write, to express herself creatively, but she has been convinced by others that that is damaging to her health. Her simple desire for activity and intellectual stimulation is met with disapproval. So "what is one to do?" (page 286).

3. From a personal point of view, John treats his wife lovingly, but like a child. She is given no credit for good sense or for emotions worth noting. She is considered a "little goose" and a "little girl." It is this very attitude on John's part that the wife finds so frustrating. His laughing at her and ignoring her real needs is precisely what has brought her to the edge of insanity. Medically, the husband has treated her in typical nineteenth century fashion. As a scientist he has studied her case, found little evidence of physical illness and proceeded to treat her accordingly. Her mental state is not to be questioned; her position as woman, not to be considered. Her illness more than partially results from this total disregard for her needs. As John continues to treat her with growing lack of comprehension of her real problems, her condition worsens irreparably.

Additional Questions

1. From whose point of view is the story narrated? To what degree does the point of view contribute to the effectiveness of the story? Could it have been told from another point of view? Explain.

    The story is told from the distraught wife's point of view. Most students will probably agree that the story's effectiveness derives from its being told by this woman who slowly descends into the maelstrom of madness. For any other character to tell the story would be to eliminate the intensity, the sense of participation and identification the reader has with this woman. Other students, however, might feel the story is almost too intense as written, and they would welcome a more objective viewpoint.

2. What contrasts can you detect in the nature or general outlook of the husband and wife? How do these contrasts contribute to the woman's deteriorating mental state?

The husband is first of all a scientist, dealing with black and white, provable issues. He sees his wife as an innocent, childlike creature to be coddled and cared for. She is supposed to exist for his benefit, to take care of herself for his sake. The wife, however, is an intelligent, thinking human being with a potential that is totally thwarted by his attitude. If, by nature, she had been a passive, submissive woman, she would have less difficulty existing within this nineteenth century view of marriage. As it is, however, she is a creative person concerned with the life of the imagination. To be treated as a child, as an unthinking dependent person, is to remove all vestiges of human worth from her.

3. Why is the wife unable to communicate her real feelings to her husband? What happens on those specific occasions when she makes a conscious attempt to talk with him?

John's patriarchal attitude toward his wife makes any attempt to communicate with him a frustrating experience for her. He laughs at her when she attempts to express her doubts. ". . . But one expects that in marriage," she comments (page 286). He calls her a "blessed little goose" (page 289) when she expresses discomfort in her surroundings. Forced into a role of subterfuge, she finds any real communication between them impossible.

4. The story has been described as one to "freeze our . . . blood." How accurate do you consider this description? What elements of horror did you find in the story?

Students might well point to the setting of the room, with its abhorrent wallpaper, barred windows, and bolted bed as trappings of a horror story. Certainly the characterization of the wife as she loses all touch with reality and enters the world of madness might well "freeze our blood."

Composition

1. Several decades before the publication of this story, Emily Dickinson wrote, "Much madness is divinest sense . . . Much sense the starkest madness." How might these words apply to the situation presented in this story?

2. The wife in "The Yellow Wallpaper" feels her health would improve if she were allowed to write. What within her personality makes writing so necessary? What role does it play in her life? What contribution toward the retention of her sanity might writing have provided?

Patterns / p. 301
Amy Lowell (1874–1925)

A simple story of unfulfilled love begins quietly enough. It ends, however, as a protest against those unnatural, artificially imposed patterns that often prevent us from fulfilling our lives. Amy Lowell, a Pulitzer Prize winner, was a member of the Imagists, a group of poets dedicated to the use of free verse, open expression of ideas, and above all, concrete and rich images.

Insight

1. The action of "Patterns" takes place in a formal garden of England during the spring of the year as "all the daffodils are blowing" (lines 2–3). The time of the poem is the eighteenth century, which was known as The Age of Reason, a period of formality in manners, dress and art. This formality of the period and the setting is echoed in the formal patterns of the speaker's life and in the poem's theme as well.

2. The young woman of the poem has received a message notifying her of her lover's death. She has taken the news with the utter emotional control expected of her. "See that the messenger takes some refreshment," (line 69) she correctly remembers to say. Her self-restraint is all part of a pattern, but a pattern she begins to question as she wanders the garden. She roams the paths conscious of the contrast between her emotions and the loveliness and gaiety of her physical surroundings. She even begins to daydream of being surprised by her lover as she bathes in the fountain. But it is one of the patterns of her life—her own stiff brocaded gown—that returns her to the reality of her own sorrow. Her sorrow is, however, turning to anger and frustration at the restraints life has placed upon her. Because of these patterns her love has not been fulfilled. "Christ! What are patterns for?" (line 107).

3. First, the pattern of the garden path, carefully arranged in formal walks is identified. The stiff, brocaded gown is another pattern as is the emotional control expected of the woman as she receives her devastating news. "I stood upright too/Held rigid to the pattern/By the stiffness of my gown" (lines 76–78). She also speaks of the expected chastity, a pattern she would have broken with Lord Hartwell. Finally, there is "a pattern called a war" (line 106), the final pattern to affect her young life. Each of these patterns is a convention, a system created by humans. They are not the natural world of flowers and breezes and sunshines. Rather, they oppress and inhibit and ultimately destroy her dreams.

Additional Questions

1. "Patterns" is famous for its brilliant and rich imagery. Find examples

that are particularly vivid to you. What effect results from the use of such striking images?

Some students may be particularly impressed by the images used to describe the woman. "In my stiff, brocaded gown./With my powdered hair and jeweled fan,/I too am a rare/Pattern" (lines 5–8). Other students will, no doubt, point to the imagery of the seasons such as "The squills and daffodils/Will give place to pillared roses, and to asters, and to snow" (lines 95–96). The imagery in the poem is particularly vivid clarifying all the details so they can be heard, seen, and felt by the reader. The overall effect of striking richness makes the poem vivid and memorable.

2. The poem is built upon contrast—specifically, contrast between the natural and the artificial. What contrasts can you find in "Patterns"? What is their effect upon the meaning of the poem?

The poem, a protest against the artificial, self-imposed patterns of our existence, is clarified for the reader by the contrasts presented. The formal gardens, the stiff brocade, the emotional restraint of the speaker are all contrasted to the life and gaiety of spring, to the freedom and loveliness of a woman bathing, even to the natural need to show one's grief.

Composition

"Christ! What are patterns for?" cries the speaker of the poem. What are they for? Do they ever serve a positive purpose or is their purpose always to restrain, to repress?

In Summary

From Sappho to Sexton the role of woman has been a clearly defined one. She has been the wife, the mother, the helper. She has been the receiver, the observer, the reflector. Sometimes, she accepted; sometimes, rebelled; sometimes, both. Bradstreet, for example, served as loving wife, devoted mother of eight. Yet in a land and an age when literature was still a luxury to a people striving to survive, she created.

For many the assigned role was confinement itself. Who can assess the unfulfilled destinies of half a world? Who might have equalled Shakespeare?

Only this can be said: The future role of women will not be that of the past. New roles have opened: old barriers have fallen. To the attainment of these ends, the writers in this unit have contributed. Their voices, eloquent and loud, have been heard. There may be roles, they say. But more importantly, there are choices.

Suggested Reading

*Carrier, Constance. *The Middle Voice*. New York: Alan Swallow, 1954.

Colette, Sidonie-Gabrielle. *Collected Works*. New York: Farrar, Straus & Cudahy.

Deutsch, Babette. *Banners*. New York: Doubleday, 1919.

Kizer, Carolyn. *Knock Upon Silence*. New York: Doubleday, 1965.

————. *The Ungrateful Garden*. Bloomington: Indiana University Press, 1961.

*Lowell, Amy. *The Complete Poetical Works of Amy Lowell*. Boston: Houghton Mifflin, 1955.

*McCarthy, Mary. *Memories of a Catholic Girlhood*. New York: Harcourt Brace Jovanovich, 1957.

McCullers, Carson. *The Ballad of the Sad Cafe and Other Stories*. Boston: Houghton Mifflin, 1951.

*McGinley, Phyllis. *The Love Letters of Phyllis McGinley*. New York: Viking Press, 1954.

Mew, Charlotte. *Collected Poems*. London: Gerald Duckworth & Co.

*Millay, Edna St. Vincent. *Collected Poems*. New York: Harper & Row, 1956.

O'Connor, Flannery. *A Good Man Is Hard To Find*. New York: Harcourt Brace Jovanovich, 1955.

————. *Everything That Rises Must Converge*. New York: Farrar, Straus & Giroux, 1965.

Olsen, Tillie. *Tell Me A Riddle*. Philadelphia: J. B. Lippincott, 1961.

Plath, Sylvia. *Ariel*. New York: Harper & Row, 1961.

Rich, Adrienne. *Leaflets*. New York: W. W. Norton, 1969.

Rukeyser, Muriel. *Waterlily Fire, Poems 1935–1962*. New York: Macmillan, 1962.

Sexton, Anne. *Love Poems*. Boston: Houghton Mifflin, 1969.

POETRY

Poems / p. 309
Sappho (600 B.C.)

Sappho, one of the greatest lyric poets of antiquity, wrote poems of deep personal feeling simply expressed with grace and delicacy. When her works were collected in the third century B.C., they filled nine books; however, most of them have been lost. Only two of her odes and fragments of a thousand or so lines survive.

If, Lord, Thy Love for Me Is Strong / p. 311
Teresa of Avila (1515–1582)

The Soul's Garment / p. 312
Margaret Cavendish (1624–1673)

Two poets from two different centuries and two different countries speak of religion and God's love.

Insight

1. The speaker in the Teresa of Avila poem displays an uncertainty not apparent in the Cavendish poem. The former speaker asks the Lord why their union has not been completed: "What holds thee, Lord, so long from me?" (line 4). Her desire is to be joined with God in love, but although she has given her love to the Lord she appears uncertain that their final union will take place as she questions just "What fears can yet assail thee now?" (line 7).
2. The speaker in the Cavendish poem appears more assured than the speaker in the Teresa of Avila poem. In the Cavendish poem there is an air of certainty and expectation. The speaker reveals no doubts concerning the eventual fate of her soul. She states that during one's lifetime the soul is clothed by "Great Nature" but Death, as a result of age and illness, removes the soul's outerwear—or human form—which is then laid to rest. The soul, however, will live again within new "fleshy garments."
3. The speaker in the Teresa of Avila poem addresses the poem to the Lord. She asks him directly what is keeping them separated from one another. Throughout the poem, the speaker's questions go unanswered. The use of apostrophe in this poem adds to the sense of immediacy and life which the poet wishes to create.

Song / p. 313
Aphra Behn (1640–1689)

I Can't Hold You and I Can't Leave You / p. 314
Sister Juana Inés de La Cruz (1651–1695)

A Song / p. 315
Anne Finch (1666–1720)

Aphra Behn, the first Englishwoman to write for money, Sister Juana, a Mexican nun, and Anne Finch, an English Countess, were all remarkable for writing at a time in history in which women's efforts were often ridiculed and opposed. In all three of the poems which follow, love is the object of their concern.

Insight

1. Behn portrays love as a victorious knight armed with such characteristics as power, desire, pride, and cruelty. The speaker sees love as a majesty so grand as to be almost unattainable. Sister Juana displays a more ambivalent feeling toward love. She can neither hold onto love, nor let it go. She can only arm herself with defenses so that part of her can adore and part abhor her love. She is seeking a protection against the feuding and jealousy that is a part of love. The speaker in the Finch poem feels the fickleness, the uncertainties of her relationship with love. Depending upon another's heart is such an uncertain state that she simply asks that "my fond Enquiries cease,/And so let all my Troubles end" (lines 13–14).
2. Love is personified as a knight armed with tyrannical power. He sits triumphant while others sit at his feet worshipping. Love, with his pride, cruelty, and desire, has been armed by God who "set him up a Deity" (line 14). The personification of love in this poem adds vitality to the poet's concept of love. Rather than a mere definition of love, she endows the emotion with traits that are meaningful and understandable to the reader.

Additional Question

Which poem do you find most effective? Which least? Explain.

Sister Juana's poem may well speak most clearly to today's audience. Certainly, many people have experienced those ambivalent feelings of loving yet wishing one could be free of love. The emotions expressed in the Finch poem are also ones familiar to many persons today. The Behn poem may appear the most remote, yet many readers will find the ideas expressed satisfying and effectively presented.

On Being Brought from Africa to America / p. 316
Phillis Wheatley (1753–1784)

Brought to Boston as a slave from Africa in 1761, Wheatley was educated and encouraged to write by the family that purchased her.

Insight

1. The speaker was an African slave brought to America. She sees herself initially as a "benighted soul," once a heathen unaware of God and Christ.
2. The "redemption" is her new knowledge of salvation that may come as a result of her belief in God and Christ. Once in America she has been converted to Christianity, and she now realizes that no matter what her color, she can "join th' angelic train" to salvation.
3. Wheatley refers to "Pagan," a religious belief in heathenism. In line three she refers to both "God" and "Savior," references to the Christian creator and His son. Line 7 of the poem includes three allusions: Christians, members of a particular religion, Negroes, a race of people, and Cain, the murderer and brother of Abel.

Sonnets from the Portuguese / p. 318
Elizabeth Barrett Browning (1806–1861)

The following selections are from *Sonnets from the Portuguese*, a collection of intensely personal love poems written by Elizabeth Barrett to Robert Browning. Before her marriage to Browning, the poet lived as an invalid and virtual prisoner in her father's house. While the new life with her husband promised love, it also raised questions in the poet's mind.

Insight

1. Browning followed the Petrarchan sonnet form in her writing. The octave of Sonnet XIV states the poet's desire to be loved for love's sake only. The sonnet closes with her hope that if loved for love's sake only, their love will be so strong as to endure for eternity. In Sonnet XXXV the speaker requests that if she is to give up everything for her love, will he, in turn, be everything to her? She summarizes her needs as she explains to her love that he will have to open his heart wide in order to be "all" to her. In Sonnet XLIII the speaker says she will enumerate all the ways she loves him. She concludes by stating that God willing, she will even love him more after death.
2. The speaker does not want to be remembered for those characteristics that are purely transitory such as her smile, her way of speaking or thinking. These, she states, may change, and if they do, his love might

change as well. Rather, she asks that he love her for the sake of love only for then their love should last through eternity.

3. The speaker will be leaving "Home-talk and blessing and the common kiss" (line 3). To go with her lover will be to conquer the familial love she has previously felt and must now leave. The grief over this loss will sorely test her new love. She wants her lover to "Open thine heart" and help her to conquer her grief which shall surely make her hard to love.

4. The speaker enumerates at least seven ways she loves. She loves him as deeply and widely as her soul can possibly love. She loves him morning, noon and night, no matter what the day may bring. She loves him freely, purely, and passionately. She loves him with her whole entity now "—and, if God choose/I shall but love thee better after death" (lines 13–14).

Composition
Develop an idea using either the Petrarchan or Shakespearian sonnet form. Write the sonnet in iambic pentameter with a definite rhyme scheme as suggested by the form chosen. Remember the division of ideas into octave and sestet or quatrains and a rhyming couplet.

Remembrance / p. 320
Emily Brontë (1818–1848)

Author of the single, but brilliant novel *Wuthering Heights*, Brontë also wrote poetry of an intense, personal nature.

Insight
1. The poet employs the poetic device of apostrophe as the speaker addresses her love who is "cold in the earth . . . cold in the dreary grave" (lines 1–2).
2. The speaker, admitting that she faithfully remembers their youthful love, tells her dead lover that a new lover has never been found. Yet, her memories of a lost love are so painful that she cannot allow herself to recall them for fear she will be unable to face the world.
3. No matter how empty her existence is now, the speaker maintains she has learned to live without joy. Not even despair, she maintains, can destroy her feeling for the importance of life—even if it is a life without joy.
4. The end rhymes in the first three stanzas are: thee, thee; grave, wave; hover, cover; shore, more; Decembers, remembers; spring, suffering.

Additional Question
The poem is an apostrophe (text page 312) to the speaker's dead love. What does the use of apostrophe contribute to the effectiveness of the poem?
By directly addressing her dead lover as if he could answer her, the

speaker leaves an impression of deep emotion as well as a feeling for the richness of life. As a result, these emotions are transferred to the reader who reacts with sympathy and understanding.

A Birthday / p. 322
Christina Rossetti (1830–1894)

In an age which did not look kindly upon women writers, Rossetti, with quiet restraint, expressed her religious and personal feelings.

Insight

1. The speaker compares her heart to a singing bird, an over-ladened apple tree, a small boat on a quiet sea. These similes convey an image of a heart so filled with joy that it can almost sing to express its utter happiness.
2. The speaker's love has come, and, as a result, her life has just begun. "The birthday of my life/Is come, my love is come to me" (lines 15–16). In her exuberance she asks for a majestic celebration with a platform carved in birds and fruit with royal colors of gold, silver and purple.

This Is My Letter to the World / p. 323
I Like a Look of Agony / p. 323
There's Been a Death in the Opposite House / p. 325
I Heard a Fly Buzz / p. 326
Emily Dickinson (1830–1886)

One of America's foremost poets, Dickinson lived an outwardly uneventful life. Although much of her poetry reflects her solitary, reclusive existence, the poetry is as vigorous and witty as it is touching and sensitive.

Insight

1. The speaker refers to her poetry as her "letter to the world." For although the world may never pay much attention to her, she wishes to share her views of the world's simplicity and majesty through her writing. This is such a vital message that she will share it with those living and those yet to be born, and she asks only "Judge tenderly—of Me" (line 8).
2. To the speaker, a look of agony, like a fit, a convulsion, or death, is an honest, natural expression of anguish. Unlike other emotions, it cannot be faked or simulated. It is not that the speaker likes to see human suffering, only that she appreciates the honesty by which some emotions are expressed.
3. It is more than intuition that tells the speaker there has been a death. The unusual parade of visitors to the house, the neighbors in and out, the doctor, the minister, the milliner and finally the undertaker all attest

to a death in the house. The "Man of the Appalling Trade" is the undertaker who sizes up the household and arranges for "that Dark Parade" (line 20).

4. The speaker is interrupted in her last moments of assigning or bequeathing her keepsakes to those who will survive her. In a time of utmost seriousness, a simple, small housefly intrudes upon the final moment of her life and becomes the last conscious thought she has. It is, indeed, an ironic ending for one's life. One would, perhaps, expect trumpets to blare or at least the wailing of mourners. Instead, a pesty, ubiquitous creature from life buzzes the speaker in her last moment. The speaker then finds "the Windows failed" (line 15). Life is shut out of her consciousness and she dies.

Additional Question

Perhaps the strongest virtue of Dickinson's writing was her ability to take a common, everyday object or a specific detail and to imbue it with vitality and life so that the smallest detail would suggest a general truth. Find examples in the above poetry of her excellent use of detail.

Students may point to the fly in "I Heard A Fly Buzz" as an example of a detail that gives substance to the poem and to its meaning. Other students may suggest that all the details of the house in which there has been a death again lead to the very meaning of the poem itself. Even so small a thing as a look, a quick look of agony, has been captured by the poet and used to illustrate a general truth.

Puritan Sonnet / p. 327
Elinor Wylie (1885–1928)

Cold Fear / p. 328
Elizabeth Madox Roberts (1886–1941)

The Pear Tree / p. 329
H.D. (Hilda Doolittle) (1886–1961)

"Oh world, I cannot hold thee close enough!" Millay exclaims in one of her most famous poems. It is a similar fascination toward this same natural world which concerns the following three poets, each of whom reveals a different attitude toward the subject.

Insight

1. The speaker in the Wylie poem is apparently someplace different from her native New England "pastures fenced with stone" (line 8). The richness of the scene she sees, contrasting sharply with the austere monotones she prefers, causes the speaker with her Puritan nature to rebel against such a luxurious setting. The setting of "Cold Fear" is a

stormy winter day. The speaker, just returning from a walk through the storm, is left with vivid impressions of the coldness and her resulting fear. In "Pear Tree" the speaker stands with arms upraised in an almost worshipful attitude to this tree whose blossoms will "bring summer and ripe fruits/in their purple hearts" (lines 15–16).

2. The most terrifying view of nature is found in "Cold Fear" with its wind that "tried to tear my clothes away./And the cold came in" (lines 7–8). Even after the speaker escapes into the warmth of the house she can still feel the cold. "I kept remembering the wind/And the cold ground" (lines 31–32). The speaker in the H.D. poem has the most appreciative view of nature. Hers is an almost reverential attitude toward the power of the process of life. Finally, "Puritan Sonnet" establishes a clear contrast between what the speaker loves (the austere New England countryside) and what she dislikes ("There's something in this richness that I hate" line 2).

3. "Cold Fear" is filled with images of all types. Images of touch such as "My face stung in the hard sleet," (line 2) images of sound such as "The ice drops rattled where there was ice," (line 9) and images of sight such as "I saw a moth wing that was dry/and thin" (lines 13–14) are all present in the poem. "Pear Tree" is built upon one effective, extended image of the tree in full blossom with its "silver dust lifted from the earth" (lines 1–2). In "Puritan Sonnet" the imagery is primarily imagery of sight describing the "landscapes drawn in pearly monotones" (line 4).

Additional Question

How do the titles "Puritan Sonnet" and "Cold Fear" contribute to the meaning of each poem?

The word "Puritan" carries with it connotations of austerity, of simplicity. Thus the title prepares the reader for the contrast that is to come.

The title "Cold Fear" starkly summarizes the two feelings that resulted from the night in the storm.

Composition

A poet uses images to make her abstract ideas and feelings concrete. Examine how two of the above poets make use of imagery. What is the particular abstract idea each image clarifies?

Still Falls the Rain / p. 330
Edith Sitwell (1887–1964)

Although much of Sitwell's poetry is light in tone, this poem with its startling images reflects the nightmare reality of World War II London in which she lived.

Insight

1. The modern event, the bombing raids of World War II on England, is, the speaker suggests, a further embodiment of the crucifixion of Christ. Centuries later the rain is still falling and the earth is as "dark," as "black," as "blind" as it ever was. Christ, "the Starved Man hung upon the Cross" (line 13) continues to bleed for "the wounds of the sad uncomprehending dark" (line 21).

2. Not only does the rain suggest the actual bombs falling upon England, but it further symbolizes the blood that has fallen as a result of the sinning, evil quality of the human race that today can bomb a city and centuries ago could crucify its supposed Savior. The rain is "dark" and "blind" to whom it falls upon and where it falls.

Additional Question

What does the repetition of the line "Still falls the rain" have upon the effect of the poem?

   A mournful, haunting quality results from the repetition of the line. Each time one is reminded that the bombs have not ceased, the blood continues to flow. But, as the poem concludes, and the last use of the word "still" emphasizes, Christ shall continue to shed his blood for the world.

Composition

Make a list of as many symbols familiar to your everyday life as possible. Choose one of these symbols and write a poem or essay in which you make use of the symbol to illustrate a larger idea.

In the Evening / p. 333
Anna Akhmatova (1889–1966)

Intimate / p. 334
Gabriela Mistral (1889–1956)

The Chilean writer and Nobel Prize winner Gabriela Mistral and the Russian poet Anna Akhmatova examine in these two poems some of the complexities of a man-woman relationship.

Insight

1. "I'm a faithful friend," (line 5) asserts the speaker's lover in the Akhmatova poem. His caress is unromantic, his eyes laugh at her. The speaker realizes these gestures as she recognizes that the violin's music appears to be mocking her relationship as it plays "the most heartbreaking songs" (line 2). In the Mistral poem the speaker portrays her lover as seeking a physical acknowledgment of their love, an acknowledgment she feels could be a lie. Rather, the speaker warns him that her

body is merely an outer shell. An outer expression of their love, like the outer shell, will be meaningless after they are dead. Rather, it is the meaning of the kiss, not the lips that should be significant in their relationship.

2. The tone of the Akhmatova poem is sarcastic and bitter. The speaker's mention of the "heartbreaking songs" of the violin is the first hint that all is not well. "How far from a caress," (line 7) she utters sarcastically. Her bitterness is reinforced in the last stanza as "the violins mourn on" (line 13). The Mistral poem conveys a less bitter, more matter-of-fact tone. The speaker desires more than the physical union offered her. In realistic terms she tells her lover, "Touch me not" (line 25) for that alone would be neither a truthful nor a total expression of their love.

Composition

To which poem did you respond most strongly? Describe your response and attempt to justify it by direct references to the poem.

Silence / p. 336
Marianne Moore (1887–1972)

Marianne Moore, over twenty years after winning the 1952 Pultizer Prize for Poetry, remains one of America's foremost poets. In this poem her unique ability to express a principle spontaneously and humorously is evident as she defines "superior people."

Insight

1. "Superior people" act with self-restraint. Capable of enjoying their solitude, they do not impose themselves on others nor do they always feel they must comment upon someone else's speech, no matter how delightful.

2. Believing in the importance of self-restraint, the speaker's father could still sincerely offer his home as a place to stay, as an inn. After all, inns are temporary locations only. People were free to visit, he implied, but only for a reasonable period of time.

Composition

What are the characteristics you consider important to "superior people"? In your definition attempt to limit yourself to one or two characteristics upon which you elaborate much as Moore has done in this poem.

A Letter / p. 337
Marina Tsvetayeva (1892–1941)

Elizabeth / p. 339
Sylvia Townsend Warner (born 1893)

Résumé / p. 340
Dorothy Parker (1893–1967)

Tsvetayeva, a Russian master of her craft, Warner, an English writer of both fiction and poetry, and Parker, a renowned writer of light but biting verse examine the subject of death from various points of view.

Insight

1. In the first lines the speaker makes clear that "they don't expect letters," but all the time "they wait for a letter." Just because people may not expect a letter doesn't mean they can help themselves from waiting for one. Similarly, these people, apparently prisoners, expect to find death, not happiness. They will receive death; but as the speaker exclaims, "It's not happiness, old girl!" (line 19). It is simply nothing but "the last dream." The use of paradox in this poem has a certain shock value that draws attention to and emphasizes the ideas presented.
2. "Elizabeth the Beloved" is carved upon an old, weatherbeaten tombstone. These are the only words that can be deciphered, and the speaker realizes that only one thing is clear: Elizabeth was once someone beloved, but now she belongs only to death.
3. Parker's poem reveals a witty if macabre attitude toward suicide. All means of killing oneself are uncomfortable, the poet implies, so "You might as well live." Warner's poem exemplifies the transitory quality of one's relationships in life. Death, however, holds the ultimate relationship for no matter how beloved one might be when alive, time shall bring one only to death. Finally, Tsvetayeva speaks of death as "the last dream" (lines 27–28) in which one's life will end abruptly, "no one's old" (lines 28–29).

The Meeting / p. 341
Louise Bogan (1897–1970)

Two people can meet day after day and develop an intense, personal relationship. Two other people can meet day after day and develop nothing but a casual acquaintanceship. These latter two are the ones Bogan concerns herself with in this poem.

Insight

1. The two have been acquaintances for years, yet their relationship has not been a particularly close one. After the initial greetings, the man has shown little interest in the speaker. The speaker realizes now that she is not part of his world nor will she ever be. Their meetings will continue, their greetings will be gay, but their relationship will never be more than a casual acquaintanceship.
2. Initially there is a rather sad, questioning tone to the poem. "I thought

I knew," (line 1) the speaker says. She seems in a quandary, somewhat confused by the man's apparent initial interest, but subsequent indifference. The tone of the poem shifts as the speaker realizes the futility of dreaming about a relationship with this man. The last two lines are surely uttered with a bitter sadness and a note of finality.

Composition
Describe a meeting you have looked forward to only to be disappointed by the moment itself. Attempt to analyze what factors were responsible for your feelings of disappointment.

To the Dark God / p. 343
Paula Ludwig (1900–1974)

In this poem the German poet Paula Ludwig describes her foreboding, yet accepting sense of being hunted by a dark God.

Insight
1. The speaker has been hiding from God. She has hidden herself in the world of nature, "green boughs hanging over me" (line 5). Yet the dark God has managed to find her almost instinctively, she feels, "with the scent of a hunter/without trap or dagger" (lines 8–9).
2. The speaker is admitting through this line and the closing line, "My hands growing toward you," that she has wanted to be found, has wanted to be traced to her hiding place on the damp forest floor. She may not have moved, but the very growth of her hands reaching towards the dark God has betrayed her presence.

Song / p. 344
Marya Zaturenska (born 1902)

Ride / p. 346
Josephine Miles (born 1911)

Zaturenska, a Russian-born American writer and winner of the Pulitzer Prize in 1938 and Miles, an American poet and writer of extensive studies on the language of poetry, see the world quite differently in these two contrasting poems.

Insight
1. Although life in the first world may be weary, it still smiles and offers "her horn/Of plenty and surprise" (lines 2–3). Yet, where the speaker was born life was filled with fear, deprivation, and greed. As a result the speaker built a new world, a dream world, for herself, but now she realizes that that romantic world is unnatural. It is "too clear,/too

luminous for joy" (lines 11–12). As a result, her dream world has dissolved and has left her with the real world "a harvest never lost" (line 20).

2. The horn of plenty might hold the surprise of an uncaring, indifferent world. In neither her present world, nor the world in which she was born, did the speaker expect to accept this vision of the world. She strove to develop another vision only to have her dreams melt and dissolve. Now she realizes she can do nothing more for the world is, in reality, harsh, unkind, and indifferent to her.

3. In the Zaturenska poem, the speaker, fearing she will be destroyed by the world, attempts to build a new world for herself. The speaker in the Miles poem, however, has not tried to change the world, has not attempted to build a dream world at all. As she rides through life she realizes that by merely living in the world she has helped make it. One may say, "It's not mine, not yours, not ours." But in reality, "it's down the road, and we're in it" (line 8). We are all a part of the world and help to make it what it is.

Additional Question

The Zaturenska poem begins using *personification* (text page 315). What is the personification? What human characteristics has this abstract idea taken on?

The speaker talks of "life" as if it were a person with the human characteristics of a "smile" and "weary eyes." As a result of using personification, the speaker's whole concept of life takes on a personal, meaningful image.

In Time Like Air / p. 346
May Sarton (born 1912)

A Belgium-born, naturalized American citizen, Sarton is a prolific writer of both poetry and fiction. In this poem she describes love through the effective use of metaphor.

Insight

1. The speaker notes that although in water salt totally disappears from sight, it is, in reality, everywhere. On the other hand, in air, salt becomes a pure crystal once again. It regains its entity, its essence.

2. In the third stanza the speaker asks if an element like air or water exists that will do for the soul what has been done for salt. That is, what element will define the soul's essence or will dissolve it "So it may be both found and lost" (line 15)?

3. Love is the element that will "in time" define one's soul. In its early stages, love is pure sensation, an intense attachment. After this, however, detachment, like the "faultlessly pure, faultlessly white" crystal

of salt may be achieved, but only in time for "In time like air is essence stated" (line 30).

4. Sarton compares the soul and its reaction to love with salt and its reaction to both air and water. Both salt and the soul, she suggests, need particular elements in which to define their essence.

Beverly Hills, Chicago / p. 348
Gwendolyn Brooks (born 1917)

The first black writer to be awarded the Pulitzer Prize, Brooks in this poem contrasts the world of plenty with the world of deprivation.

Insight

1. The speaker is, presumably, a black person, taking a ride in a neighborhood much richer, more luxuriant than her own.
2. The neighborhood in which the speaker is driving is a world of "golden gardens," (line 3) where even the leaves fall in lovely patterns and the garbage "is a neat brilliancy" (line 8). The people move gently and slowly "touched by that everlasting gold" (line 10). The speaker comes from a poorer neighborhood where tea is not "served" but just fixed with "the juice of the cheapest lemons that are sold" (line 13). In her neighborhood one assumes "the summer ripeness rots . . . raggedly" (line 6) and the garbage is not neat at all.
3. It is not that she wants what these people have for she realizes they have their troubles although "it is trouble with a gold-flecked beautiful banner" (line 20), and they too shall die although they do often "live till their hair is white" (line 24). She does, however, contrast her world to their world and feels the inequity of it all. Their worlds are so far apart, "it is only natural that we should think we have not enough" (line 35).
4. In the second stanza, "ripeness rots . . . raggedly" is an example of alliteration as is the repetition of "s" sounds in the next stanza in "sweetly . . . softness and slowness." In the fourth stanza "beautiful banner" and in the fifth stanza "passings . . . painful" and "excellent . . . expensive" are all examples of alliteration.

The Centaur / p. 350
May Swenson (born 1919)

Swenson, a contemporary American poet, has often been praised for the joyful, imaginative quality of her poetry. It is this very quality that is predominant in "The Centaur."

Insight

1. It was her tenth summer in which she played her game of centaur.

The speaker would carve an imaginary horse from a willow branch and spend her day trotting and cantering "along in the lovely dust" (line 19). It is a memory so vivid to the speaker that it is hard for her to believe it was so long ago and that it lasted for only one summer.

2. Her mother is concerned about her daughter's appearance, not about her daughter's imaginary game. "Go tie back your hair," her mother suggests (line 61). It is as if she were to say, "Grow up, why are you involved in child's play?" It may have been a long time since the speaker "swished through the dust," (line 37) yet to her the memory is almost as vivid as if she had played the game yesterday.

3. "Snorted" and "swished" are onomatopoetic words referring to sounds the imaginary horse makes. "The wind twanged" is another example of onomatopoeia.

Additional Question

In what way is the poem illustrative of the allusion to the Greek Centaurs?

The allusion is to the fabled race of creatures who were half human and half horse. In this poem the speaker, although human, takes on the characteristics of a horse as she canters and trots in the dust. "My hair flopped to the side . . . (line 29). My forelock swung in my eyes . . . (line 31). I shied and skittered and reared,/stopped and raised my knees,/ pawed at the ground and quivered" (lines 33–35).

The Alarm Clock / p. 353
Mari Evans

In this poem a black poet describes a person's awakening to her own blackness.

Insight

1. Both wakings have been rude and abrupt. The shrillness of an alarm ringing is an unpleasant, brisk way to start the day. The clerk's words were just as unpleasant and brisk, and they, too, were an awakening for the speaker. As the speaker says of that day in the drugstore, "I woke up quick like I did this mornin' " (lines 21–23).

2. The speaker awakens to her own blackness in the drug store when the clerk says, "I'm sorry but we don't serve you people here" (lines 17–20). Seemingly pleasant details such as the clerk's yellow hair, her smile, the speaker's mind roaming "far off" contribute to the shock the speaker feels as she hears the devastating words.

The Gardener to His God / p. 354
Mona Van Duyn (born 1921)

May 10th / p. 356
Maxine Kumin (born 1925)

Two contemporary American poets examine nature from their unique points of view.

Insight

1. The speaker, a gardener, has read an advertisement that alleges the act of prayer will make "flowers grow many times faster, stronger, larger." If this is true, she sees a disorder, a disproportion of nature to the rest of the world—particularly to the world of the heart. It is love, she says, that needs the spaciousness, love that should grow "faster, stronger, larger." Everything else in the world, including the flowers in a gardener's world, must exist within limits.
2. The speaker in the Kumin poem chooses obscure, but fascinating aspects to illustrate nature's process of birth and development. The miraculous quality of the natural world is emphasized in the images of the fiddleheads, the new-born bat, and the tadpoles. The speaker's attitude is clearly revealed in her exclamation, "I mean walk softly" (line 13). All these incredible natural processes are, she implies, going on around us. Thus do not disturb the miraculous rebirth of spring.
3. The imagery in the Kumin poem is far from the typical buttercups and red tulips of some poets. Kumin writes of fiddleheads and tadpoles, of a shrew and a bat. These realistic images emphasize the miraculous quality of the life cycle. Indeed, one does want to "walk softly" for the poem has awakened our sensitivity to the natural world about us. Van Duyn relies almost wholly on images of sight, yet, her images are sharply drawn and uniquely expressed. She asks, for example, that "bleedingheart hang in its old way" (line 3) and "old oaks color the fall sky" (line 4) and "no rose . . . send up a swollen face" (lines 4–5).

Composition

Write a short description, prose or poetry, of a particular aspect of nature. Choose images that are appropriate yet are also uniquely descriptive of the aspect you are describing.

Further Notes for the Alumni Bulletin / p. 357
Patricia Cumming (born 1932)

Patricia Cumming lives in Boston and teaches in the writing program at Massachusetts Institute of Technology. Her poetry has appeared in numerous poetry journals, and she has published one volume of poetry.

Insight

1. The speaker expected to be able to run a beautiful, efficient household, where the silver would be polished, the car and watches would work, and fear—"the faceless dark, the sticky cobwebs in the hall" (lines 12–14)—would disappear because of love. But in reality, the household is full of dirty ashtrays and tarnished silver, and there is still a "darkness" which even "love could not lighten" (lines 30–31).

2. Early in the poem the speaker expresses her expectation that she would "have children" (line 4). The tone of this phrase suggests that having children is a convention just like getting married or having dinner parties. But at the end of the poem, the children are real people, who emerge from the troubled house in the morning to go to school. The speaker expresses her concern about them by her observation that the children "wait, silent now" (lines 32–33).

Composition

Write a composition in which you contrast the attitude toward conventional marriage in this poem and the attitude expressed in Phyllis McGinley's poem, "The 5:32" on page 284.

On Seeing My Great-Aunt in a Funeral Parlor / p. 359
Diana Chang (born 1934)

"The pain of joy is life" states the speaker in this poem by Chang. It is a life, however, in which the ceremonies of weddings and funerals become enmeshed.

Insight

1. The poem speaks of a funeral and a wedding. Both are ceremonial events; both mark beginnings—one in life, one in death.

2. The poet, paradoxically, sees death as a beginning, not as an ending. Death, the speaker implies, is a birth, a new life that results in "the pain of joy" (line 24).

Additional Question

What legacy has the great-aunt left the speaker?

The legacy is that "She leaves us listening/Her speech is young somewhere" (lines 17–18). Just as her dead body will nourish the soil from which new growth will emerge, so her dead voice has left words to be understood and heeded.

Composition

The poem is built on startling images. What, for example, are the "hotels of death"? Identify other images you find particularly effective and describe what it is about each image that helps to convey a particular feeling or thought.

A Dream / p. 361
Bella Akhmadulina (born 1937)

The modern Russian poet Akhmadulina is noted for her poetic expression of inner freedom.

Insight

1. The speaker dreams that she has returned to a home in which she once lived. She speaks with the owner; she walks in the room she once inhabited.
2. The speaker fears that she may die alone, poor, and deserted as the man in the dream remembers she did one hundred years earlier.

Eden Is a Zoo / p. 362
Margaret Atwood (born 1939)

In this poem Atwood, a Canadian writer, draws startling images in her description of a self-created world.

Insight

1. The garden is a mythical Eden, a zoo, in which the speaker has put her parents in order to protect them. Her parents are innocent souls living in a world thirty years past, a world made possible by the speaker who built it "with so much time/and pain" (lines 26–27).
2. The speaker wonders if her parents are confused when they find reminders of their past life and if they are bothered by the endless repetition of their present life. "Are they content?/Do they want to get out?" (lines 21–22). Finally, the speaker wonders if they can see her in her own world. The unanswered questions are uttered sadly, almost mournfully, by the speaker. The reader feels the speaker knows she has built such a protective garden of Eden, a paradise, that her parents are content. It is the speaker who has actually expressed her doubts. For she is the one who has separated herself and stands alone "looking at them/from across the hedge of spikes/and cardboard fire painted red" (lines 23–25).
3. In the first stanza a surrealistic garden of green sponges, lumpy trees, and a lopsided sun all give the impression of a fantasy land, a storybook world. This impression is reinforced by the caricature figures of the second stanza. The third stanza, however, brings us back to the real world, in this case, a world of familiar objects. The last image of the poem, "the hedge of spikes/cardboard fire painted red" (lines 24–25) symbolizes the separation between the two generations, a separation both painful and permanent.

In Summary

Poetry is a unique kind of language that asks much of a reader. To that reader who makes the special effort, it gives much in return. Because poets employ figurative language, that is, language that cannot be read literally, some knowledge of poetic devices is necessary. To be alert to metaphor, simile, imagery, personification, for example, is to begin to understand and appreciate poetry.

In addition, the reader must always remember that every poem projects a human voice, a speaker. The voice may be, for example, a voice of anguish or perhaps one of exuberance. Whatever emotion it carries, however, it is a voice that initially must be sought and one that inevitably cannot be denied. While the voices in this unit are all voices of women, they speak from many centuries, from common but separate hearts.

Suggested Reading

Akhmadulina, Bella. *Fever and Other New Poems.* New York: Morrow, 1969.

Akhmatova, Anna. *Selected Poems of Anna Akhmatova.* London: Oxford University Press, 1969.

Atwood, Margaret. *Procedures for Underground.* Toronto: Oxford University Press, 1970.

Bogan, Louise. *Blue Estuaries: Poems.* New York: Farrar, Straus & Giroux, 1968.

*Brontë, Emily. *Complete Poems.* New York: Columbia University Press, 1941.

*Brooks, Gwendoyn. *Selected Poems.* New York: Harper & Row, 1963.

*Browning, Elizabeth Barrett. *Complete Poetical Works.* Boston: Houghton Mifflin, 1974.

*Dickinson, Emily. *The Complete Poems of Emily Dickinson.* Boston: Little, Brown, 1960.

*H.D. (Hilda Doolittle). *Trilogy.* New York: New Directions, 1973.

Kumin, Maxine. *Up Country: Poems of New England.* New York: Harper & Row, 1972.

*Miles, Josephine. *Poems: 1930–1960.* Bloomington: Indiana University Press, 1960.

Mistral, Gabriela. *Selected Poems of Gabriela Mistral.* Bloomington: Indiana University Press, 1957.

Moore, Marianne. *Complete Poems of Marianne Moore.* New York: Viking Press, 1967.

*Parker, Dorothy. *The Portable Dorothy Parker.* New York: Viking Press, 1973.

*Roberts, Elizabeth Madox. *Under the Tree.* New York: Viking Press, 1950.

*Rossetti, Christina. *Selected Poems of Christina Rossetti*. New York: Macmillan, 1970.

Sarton, May. *A Durable Fire: New Poems*. New York: W.W. Norton, 1972.

*Sitwell, Edith. *Collected Poems*. New York: Vanguard Press, 1954.

Swenson, May. *Half Sun, Half Sleep*. New York: Scribner's, 1967.

Tsvetayeva, Marina. *Selected Poems*. London: Oxford University Press, 1971.

Van Duyn, Mona. *Merciful Disguises: Published and Unpublished Poems*. New York: Atheneum, 1973.

*Warner, Sylvia Townsend. *Time Importuned*. New York: Viking Press, 1928.

*Wheatley, Phillis. *Poems of Phillis Wheatley*. Chapel Hill: University of North Carolina, 1966.

*Wylie, Elinor. *Collected Poems*. New York: Alfred A. Knopf, 1932.

Zaturenska, Marya. *Collected Poems*. New York: Viking Press, 1965.

Breaking Free

A New England Nun / p. 367
Mary E. Wilkins Freeman (1852–1930)

When awarded the William Dean Howells Medal for Distinction in Fiction, Freeman was praised for having created "an unparalleled record of New England life." Her characters are often solitary, reclusive spinsters, but as in the case of Louisa Ellis in this story, they are also strong-willed, serene individuals, happy in the lives they have chosen to live.

Insight

1. Louisa has lived a quiet, solitary life for the past fourteen years. Settling herself into familiar patterns of behavior and living that are now threatened by her forthcoming marriage, Louisa had lived a life "full of a pleasant peace" (page 371). There was time to use her still, time to clean her house, time to sew and re-sew.

2. Because Louisa was outwardly much the person she had been when Joe left, he was once again attracted to her. Inwardly, however, Louisa has become the quintessence of an old maid, fixed in her ways, worried about changes, and upset by trifles. Only with time does Joe realize that Louisa is not the carefree young woman he left. "... finally it seemed to him that although the winds sang always that one song, it had another name" (page 371). The name was now Lily, and although Joe yearned for her, he was too honorable to break his engagement to Louisa.

3. To Louisa, Joe is the cause of change in her well-patterned existence. She realizes she would no longer be able to use her still, re-sew a seam for the pure joy of the labor, or even enjoy the immaculate cleanliness of her own home. Joe appears unaware of these feelings. He is left only perplexed and nervous around Louisa. "If he could have known it, it would have increased his perplexity and uneasiness, although it would not have disturbed his loyalty in the least" (page 370).

4. "Honor's honor, an' right's right," Lily Dyer tells Joe (page 376). This belief is exactly what keeps Joe and Louisa from breaking off their long relationship. Both are unhappy with the impending marriage, yet both feel they have made a commitment that cannot be broken. As Louisa says, "It was not for her, whatever come to pass, to prove untrue and break his heart" (page 375). At the same time Joe tells Lily that "I ain't going back on a woman that's waited for me fourteen years, an' break her heart" (page 376). Their honor is at stake, and only when Louisa becomes aware that their relationship is built upon a false premise of love, can she do the truly honorable thing and break the engagement.

5. Most students will probably agree that the title is especially appropriate to the story. Louisa, a woman of solid character and serene exterior, is the New England Nun. She chooses to live the celibate life, prayerfully thankful in her knowledge that she has control over each day. While a nun she may be, she is an uncloistered one.

Additional Questions

1. Through the use of small details, Freeman carefully portrays the developing conflicts between Louisa and Joe. Cite some specific details which you found revealing in discovering their conflicts.

    Many students may point to those details in the scene where Joe and Louisa are together. As Joe replaces the album incorrectly and leaves dirt behind as he departs, Louisa's nervousness and discomfort at having him around become clear. He changes things in her patterned existence; such changes are confusing and upsetting to this woman who has lived for fourteen years in a very cloistered, solitary manner. Other students may point to the couple's difference of opinion over the dog, Caesar, and to the conflict which must naturally arise over Louisa's realization that Joe's mother will not be happy with her still or her practice sewing.

2. In what way are Freeman's descriptions of Joe as "an innocent and perfectly well-intentioned bear" and Louisa as "the kind-hearted, long-suffering owner of the china shop" accurate and effective?

    Most students will point out that these statements describe the essence of the two characters and of their relationship. Both Louisa and Joe are good people, with good intentions. Both suffer, however, as a result of their very goodness for neither is willing to hurt the other by breaking off their relationship. Louisa tries, like the shopkeeper, to be patient and kind. Yet she worries over her belongings as big, kind-hearted Joe intrudes upon her home. On his part, Joe, "afraid to stir lest he should put a clumsy foot or hand through the fairy web," (page 370) believes he must do the honorable thing and fulfill his promise of fourteen years ago.

3. To what extent throughout the story is Louisa aware that "her feet had turned into a path, smooth maybe under a calm, serene sky, but so straight and unswerving that it could only meet a check at her grave, and so narrow that there was no room for anyone at her side"?

    From the very beginning of their engagement Louisa may very well have suspected that her acquiescence to Joe was not exactly what she wanted. She became engaged because her mother had pointed out the advantages. ". . . She had seen marriage ahead as a reasonable feature and a probable desirability of life" (page 370). Yet upon Joe's return fifteen years later, Louisa's first emotion was one of consternation. She had created a secure, happy existence for herself, and it would be difficult, indeed, to include someone else in her solitary ways. Even so, the marriage had seemed the "inevitable conclusion of things" (page 371), and Louisa simply accepted that conclusion. She did so not without sadness, however, for the life she had carved seemed all the more dear to her as she faced leaving it. In truth, Louisa is not aware that her way of living is so established that Joe can never be a part of it. If Lily and Joe had not been overheard, Louisa would have married Joe and attempted to fit into his existence, and he into hers.

4. Do you think Lily is right when she says to Joe, "You and I have got common sense"? Does Louisa have "common sense"?

    Most students will feel that none of the characters has common sense. These students will suggest that choosing to live unhappily, not even attempting to fulfill one's desires, is not a common sense approach to life. Unhappiness and frustration can only result. The characters should have examined their relationship, expressed their misgivings. Such behavior would have been the "common sense" approach. Other students will feel, however, that only Louisa displayed common sense. Louisa is the only character who is willing to change the fate of all three individuals, creating a happy circumstance for all.

Composition

Compare and contrast the personalities, characters and values of Louisa and Joe.

The Solitary / p. 379
Sara Teasdale (1884–1933)

To be "self-complete as a flower or a stone," to have attained the solitary serenity of the speaker in this poem represents a common goal but a rare accomplishment.

Insight

1. The speaker is a "self-complete" individual. She knows who she is, and she is happy with her being. Once it was important to her "to share myself with every comer/Or shape my thoughts into words with my tongue" (lines 3–4). Now as long as she has the will to enjoy and find meaning in the natural world about her, she feels that she needs no one else. Others, however, are welcome to intrude upon her solitary existence if they must, for perhaps others need her and her love, even if she needs no one.

2. Perhaps in years past those words might have described the speaker. Now, however, she is at peace with her solitude for as she says, "My heart has grown rich with the passing of years" (line 1).

Additional Question

Describe the mood of the poem. Which words or phrases are particularly effective in helping to create this mood?

The mood is one of quiet but joyous self-understanding. The speaker feels "rich" with her self-knowledge, and her feeling of pride runs throughout the poem. It is not, however, an arrogant pride for she speaks of the years that she needed others to talk to in order to shape her own thoughts. Her need is still not altogether gone, perhaps, but "I have less need now than when I was young" (line 2), she says proudly. And finally she almost shouts out to the world to think what it likes if it need to for "what is it to me/Who am self-complete as a flower or a stone" (lines 11–12).

Titty's Dead and Tatty Weeps / p. 380
Ursula MacDougall

Ursula MacDougall uses the stream-of-consciousness technique most convincingly in this story of a woman's struggle to free herself from the bonds of her own personality.

Insight

1. Others have seen Susan as the shy, mousy sister of the outgoing, gay Sally. "Miss Susan's the quiet one" (page 382), was an oft repeated refrain. And she had been quiet, but unwillingly so. She felt she could have laughed and entertained their friends, but Sally was always doing it first. "There's only room for one really free person in any family, I suppose, and Sally chose that role for herself" (page 382).
2. Sally was the dominating sister whose views and thoughts ruled the household. It was, for example, her decision on food and furnishings that was respected. Susan's point of view never particularly mattered to Sally or to others, and even Susan admits that "I never opened my mouth except to agree with her" (page 383). The sisters' relationship has left Susan dominated and repressed. After her sister's death Susan felt a sense of relief at her new-found freedom. She could now become the person she has always wanted to be. Even before the funeral she felt not sadness, only strength. "It may have been her strength that went into me. Even at the funeral I wasn't unhappy" (page 381).
3. Immediately upon Sally's death, Susan found a source of new strength. She changed the furniture around; she fired the housekeeper; she went to Bermuda. Instead of being shy and retiring, she made decisions for herself. "I'm like Sally, but only when people like Sally aren't around" (page 382). She had lived in Sally's shadow for many years, yet relieved of that shadow, she exercised her own personality and will. It is not, however, a lasting change. When faced by people who knew both sisters, Susan can no longer take on Sally's personality or be, as Susan said, "myself and Sally too." Because her new personality is just an

imitation of her sister's personality that she admired and coveted, it is unconvincing in front of familiar people. Susan returns to the shy, spineless individual she was previously.

4.   Students will probably suggest that the person she might have been, as Susan sees it, is the person Sally was. That, primarily, was Susan's wish. Some students will feel that Sally was just too domineering a person and that Susan was right to feel there wasn't room in the house for more than one with her personality. Other students, however, will point out that it is Susan's own fault that she was so dominated by her sister. Had she been a stronger person, she might have broken free from Sally and established her own personality and life.

5.   As Ella and Martha approach the house, Susan panics. She wants to avoid them and wishes she could change things back the way they were. Upon talking to them, Susan makes one attempt at preserving her new-found self as she suggests they think over Ella's plan. But Ella and Martha's persistence is enough to break Susan's resolve, and she concludes, "Well, I suppose it doesn't matter, much" (page 385). It, of course, matters a great deal, but Susan is unable to maintain her imitation of Sally because "I'm like Sally, but only when people like Sally aren't around" (page 382). Sally is, of course, still "around" in the memory of her friends.

Additional Questions

1.   Trace the relevance and effect of "Titty Mouse and Tatty Mouse" to the events of the story. What is the particular significance of the story's final reference to the nursery tale?

   At first only a few lines from the nursery tale come back to Susan. As she remembers the tale, it is clear that both Sally and Titty have been killed in an accident, that Titty Mouse and Tatty Mouse had a relationship much like Susan's and Sally's. Throughout the story, however, Susan remembers only fragments of the nursery tale, fragments that come to her mind because of an immediate action or thought. But after she has capitulated to Ella's and Martha's plan, Susan allows herself to recall the end of the tale. "—The words keep crowding down on me, faster. There's no need to go on shoving them out of my mind . . ." (page 386). And what she has tried to shove out of her mind is that in the end, Tatty, like Susan herself, is buried and suffocated by those around her.

2.   The story is written in the stream-of-consciousness technique (text page 19). How effective do you feel the technique is to this particular story? In what significant way would Susan's feelings and behavior have been distorted had the story been told from any other point of view?

   Most students will agree that this technique allowed Susan's thoughts, emotions, and dreams to be revealed. Further, these revelations are intensified and personalized because the story is told just as she is living it. The seemingly extraneous thoughts add convincing realism and are obviously not extraneous at all. Some students may disagree. They may feel that had the story been told from the third person or the omniscient point of view, it would have gained an added dimension of objectivity that it now lacks. It is this very objectivity, however, that would, no doubt, distort the characterization of Susan and result in a much weaker portrayal.

Composition

Each person at some time or other experiments with different personalities. It is a natural part of finding who we are or breaking free from how we have been viewed by others. Describe a situation in which you sought to assume a different personality. How successful were you? How lasting was the change?

Sonnet 67 / p. 387
Edna St. Vincent Millay (1892–1950)

A Wish / p. 388
Fanny Kemble (1809–1893)

Two poets from different centuries present two divergent views on the subject of immortality. Which is of greater lasting significance—the name or the deed?

Insight

1. The speaker in the Millay poem is a feminist, an activist. "I, that was proud and valiant" (line 5) she says of herself. Later she speaks of her "adventurous will." The speaker in "A Wish" defines herself much less clearly. Her interest instead is in her fame, her fear is that she may be forgotten after her death. Both wish to be remembered but in different ways.
2. In "A Wish" the speaker practically begs not to be forgotten. It is not that she wants people to mourn for her, rather she wants people to keep her memory alive. If they remember her fame and her glory, then, she feels, she will be immortalized. The speaker in Millay's sonnet, however, is more realistic. She knows she may well be forgotten as a person. Her hope is that her deeds, her "adventurous will" will be remembered and will serve as an inspiration for others to "Take up the song, forget the epitaph" (line 14).

Additional Question

What is the attitude toward death expressed in each poem? What details or images clarify this attitude? With which attitude do you feel most closely allied?

Some students may be sympathetic toward the attitude expressed in "A Wish." Here the speaker talks of the "cold earth," and the grave's "hideous arms." Death is, indeed, to this speaker a bleak, awful fate especially if the possibility of being forgotten exists. Other students will agree with Millay's poem. Here death is viewed more matter-of-factly, a recognized fate which may silence a person, may return her to dust, but a fate that can still be overcome. If one's spirit and ideas are accepted or at least recognized, then one "Can cheat the mildew and the red-brown rust" (line 11).

The Condemned Librarian / p. 389
Jessamyn West (born 1907)

Many women dream of breaking free; some actually do so; others do so, only to have the dream shatter. In this story West incisively portrays two women with similar backgrounds and dreams whose lives become enmeshed and whose destinies become interlocked.

Insight
1. Miss McCullars spent six happy years at the Liberty School. During that time she taught the children, competed with them in their games, and found time to fulfill her own interest in painting. In return, she enjoyed the admiration and friendship of those around her even though they were only "country people." But as her students began to marry and to return with their babies to visit a seemingly ageless but actually older Miss McCullars, she began to realize that "this schoolteaching was just a way of making money, of helping my mother, who was a widow" (page 392). Feeling restless and dissatisfied, she decides she could accomplish more with her life than what was possible at Liberty School.
2. "I was gambling everything on an egotistical attention-seeking whim" (page 393), Miss McCullars says of her decision to resign. She was fearful of the unknown, of a future as yet unplanned. But her mother offered her a simple solution in the form of the state college. This panacea for Miss McCullars meant she could leave home, "go to a real city, be surrounded with people devoted to learning, but not risk everything" (page 394).
3. From the very beginning, Miss McCullars has been a difficult patient. Her jealousy of a woman who has managed to change her life and fulfill her dreams has stood between the usual patient-doctor relationship. As a result, Miss McCullars is unable to identify her pains; she experiences a false sense of health that makes it next to impossible for the doctor to treat her. It is as if she were daring the doctor to diagnose her illness. ". . . Something unconscious happened the minute I crossed that threshold, something electric—and ironic" (page 398). The

"exuberance and well-being" she assumes in the office is a direct result of her challenge to the doctor in this life-and-death struggle. It is also part of her own feeling of inadequacy about her ability to make a similar radical change in her life as the doctor has successfully made in hers.

4. The battle between these two women has been a battle for superiority. The doctor, simply wishing to cure her obstinate patient, has lost the immediate battle. Miss McCullars, needing to feel superior to a woman who has accomplished what she herself is finding impossible to accomplish, may have won the immediate battle. She has lost, however, the ultimate battle, for her illness will provide an excuse for her to return to her former life, unchanged. In view of the final situations in which each woman is found, there probably has not been a winner at all. Each woman loses.

5. Dr. McKay has returned now to the nondescript, mousy librarian she had been before. Many students will probably feel that Dr. McKay is justified in accusing Miss McCullars of attempting to kill herself in order to punish the doctor for her accomplishments. Other students may feel that the doctor simply was not good enough at her profession and should have been able to treat the patient even without her cooperation. These students may point to the doctor's manner and style of dress as hints that she was too concerned with matters other than medicine.

Additional Questions

1. With what attitude does the narrator approach Dr. McKay? How do you account for this attitude?

    The narrator approached Dr. McKay with a cynical and challenging attitude. She could not allow herself to appear weak in front of this woman, nor was she going to allow this admired and worshiped doctor to triumph over her. Miss McCullars' jealousy and resentment constantly interfere with the doctor's treatment of her.

2. What parallels exist between Dr. McKay's background and current success and Miss McCullars' background and future hopes? To what extent does the narrator appear to be aware of these parallels?

    Both the doctor and Miss McCullars were once involved in education, the doctor as a librarian and the narrator as a teacher. Both had dreamed of breaking free from their profession and accomplishing more with their lives. Both had managed to take that initial step toward achieving a new life. In addition the doctor had attained the profession to which she aspired. She had totally changed her appearance, her image, her existence. Miss McCullars, rather than risk everything, makes only a partial change in her life. Even that change to a college setting to study education is not successful. She finds herself friendless, disenchanted with the people around her, and fearful of what is ahead. While not outwardly admitting to the parallels in their respective lives, the narrator may well sense them subconsciously. Certainly to a great extent her behavior towards Dr. McKay is determined by these parallels.

3. Explain the meaning of the final paragraph. What feelings of satisfaction does the narrator experience? How would you characterize her on the basis of these feelings?

The narrator's feelings of satisfaction are totally selfish ones. She was happy to have someone across the mountains sharing her own fate: the inability to fulfill her ambitions. Feeling justified in quitting the battle, she takes pleasure in knowing that she has company in her failure. "We can't all escape; some of us must stay home and do the homely tasks, however much we may have dreamed of painting or doctoring," she rationalizes (page 405). It is impossible for Miss McCullars to see the dissimilarities in their cases. The doctor, trained and successful at her second profession, has been ruined as a result of Miss McCullars' half-hearted attempt to change her own life. The doctor's struggle had been long and difficult; Miss McCullars, on the other hand, was never willing to "risk everything" and readily agreed to her mother's suggestion for a change that was not what she really dreamed of at all.

Composition

1. Describe the relationship between the narrator and her mother. Cite specific examples which show the influence of the mother on her daughter.
2. Analyze some situation in which you felt envy for another person. To what degree were your feelings based on the strengths of the other person as opposed to the weakness you may have perceived in yourself?

Advice to a Girl / p. 406
Sara Teasdale (1884–1933)

Sara Teasdale, in her clear, fresh diction, offers in this poem kindly advice to an angry, young girl. In doing so, the poet evokes a fresh look at a particular truth worth understanding and remembering.

Insight

1. Most students will probably agree that this is good advice for an independent spirit is an important asset. To own someone or to be owned by someone else may well mean, as the speaker suggests, that the person is not really worth possessing at all. Only that which is independent, its own being, is worth possessing and that never can "be quite possessed."
2. The speaker is advising a young girl who is upset and angry. Some students may suggest that the girl has been rejected in her attempt to "possess" someone. As a result, the speaker shares with the girl "This

truth, this hard and precious stone:" (line 5) anyone worth possessing will never really allow herself to be possessed. The girl should hold this truth, gaze at it, become familiar with it. Perhaps then she will understand that possession is not a goal to which she should aspire.

Additional Question

Sara Teasdale's use of metaphor (text page 347) contributes effectively to the poem's meaning. What is the metaphor she develops? What does it contribute to the meaning of the poem?

The extended metaphor that Teasdale develops is the metaphor of the truth as a stone to be touched and held and gazed at. In describing the truth as "hard," "precious," and "icy" the speaker makes it clear that this truth is, indeed, something special. It may not be easy to grasp the truth's meaning, but once understood ". . . you will be blessed" (line 11).

The Ring / p. 407
Isak Dinesen (1883–1962)

The nineteen years of Lise's fairy-tale existence have left her unprepared for the four minutes of reality that confront her. Yet, in those few minutes, she finds within herself the strength and independence to carry not only the moment but to change forever the delicate balance between her husband and herself.

Insight

1. After fighting against the wishes of her "haughty parents" for ten years, Sigismund, and Lise in particular, must feel a let down now that their marriage is a reality. Instead of the dramatic, romantic events of the past years, replete with love letters and secret meetings, they now have the mundane routine of daily existence with which to contend. "Their distant paradise had descended to earth" . . . (page 407). Lise, brought up in wealth and position, still sees life from a romantic vision. Although she approaches her tasks "gravely and solicitously," she is still living partly in a fairy-tale world where "all the time one knew one was playing" (page 407). As a result, the marriage has a quality of unreality and anti-climax to it. The young, hard-working sheep breeder, however, still adores his wife and continues to treat her as a princess.

2. This rendition of a gruesome and gory tale appeals to Lise's sense of the romantic, of the bizarre. To her the events come from the fairy-tale world of "Little Red Ridinghood" rather than from the real world in which they occur. It is this make-believe world she still seeks to exist in rather than the real world of breakfast and dogs and sheep.

3. Lise is motivated by her desire to play out a fairy tale. Once again she would be the sought-after princess, once again the center of the universe, and Sigismund "would realize what a void, what an unendurably sad and horrible place the universe would be when she was no longer in it" (page 409). How he will appreciate Lise when she returns!

4. Lise has changed. For the first time in her life she has faced a fearful, horrifying reality and won. She has exercised her will, her authoritativeness, and she has been victorious. By her very manner and actions she has stopped the thief from harming her. She has displayed a strength and a will that not even she knew existed. In realizing her strength and independence, she now sees herself as no longer merely the obedient, submissive wife. She is now aware of her own power as an individual. The fairy-tale years of dreaming of and waiting for her protective prince to come and carry her off are over.

Additional Questions

1. Lise feels "turned away by an impatient husband to whom his sheep meant more than his wife." Why do you suppose Lise feels this way? How accurate do you think this judgment is?

    Lise is so accustomed to being the center of everyone's existence that this well-intentioned act by her husband leaves her feeling rejected. The sheep, she feels, have come between them. Her romantic, self-centered character has probably caused her to overreact to her husband's telling her to go home. At the same time, however, the experience proves a "sweet" one to her. The unique quality of a day spent looking at the sheep and then being turned away, are to Lise almost moments of excitement, of unreality. She has never been treated to such mundane moments, and "she could not remember that she had ever before in all her life been altogether alone" (page 409).

2. The four minutes in the grove with the thief are of great significance to Lise's life. "During that time something happened, things were changed." What has happened? What is changed?

    During those dramatic moments Lise has been faced with a grim, fearful reality. Rather than flee or call out to her husband for help, she confronts the evil alone and through her own inner resources, defeats it. Never before was she aware that she had such strength and power. Never again will she need to depend on her husband for protection. A delicate balance in their relationship has changed forever.

3. What does the lost ring symbolize in terms of the marriage between Sigismund and Lise? How do you think their relationship will be altered as a result?

    In leaving the wedding ring behind her in the grove, Lise sheds the bonds of obedience she felt had been necessary and desirable. She has become her own person, not a fairy-tale princess and not a wife who would obey her husband in everything. She realizes she has a will of her own, a life of her own. She begins exercising this will as she lies to her husband after he asks if she knows where she lost her ring. "No," she replies to him. "I have no idea at all" (page 412).

Composition

Very few people encounter life-and-death moments of crisis as has Lise. Yet, in every life moments of crisis occur. For most people these moments become, in a sense, moments of truth. Through them, we learn our strengths or our weaknesses. Describe some such moment from your own life and what the moment revealed to you about yourself.

For My People / p. 413
Margaret Walker (born 1915)

Novelist and poet, Margaret Walker effectively portrays in this poem the frustration and anguish of black people. Raising her sympathetic but forthright voice against prejudice and hypocrisy, Walker envisions a new world to come in which "a bloody peace" shall be attained.

Insight

1. The speaker cries out against the slavery of her people who are "never gaining never reaping never knowing and/never understanding" (lines 9–10). She laments the years of schooling that simply result in the realization that because they were black and poor, "nobody cared and nobody wondered and nobody/understood" (lines 21–22). She protests her people's poverty, their present inequitable position as human beings, their frustration as they are "shackled/and tangled among ourselves by the unseen creatures/who tower over us omnisciently and laugh" (lines 37–39).
2. Not without bloodshed or revolution can this new world be born, implies the poet. She speaks of "a bloody peace," "martial songs," and in the "final clenching" there will be "the pulsing in our spirits and our blood." Once attained, however, freedom-loving inhabitants will live without prejudice, hypocrisy, or hate. The inequities that presently exist, the speaker implies, will all be remedied.

What Are Years? / p. 416
Marianne Moore (1887–1972)

A poet of unusual distinction and immensely varied interests from baseball to buffaloes, Marianne Moore never hesitated to let her moral voice be heard. In this poem she clearly speaks of life as a moral or ethical experience and further explains just what a human being's responsibility is.

Insight

1. In the first stanza the speaker begins by questioning what is a person's goodness and what is an individual's badness. Because people are "naked" or merely mortals, the speaker suggests that both good and evil exist within them. Further, she questions the source of human courage in view of living a life filled with guilt and innocence. Where, she asks, does one find the courage to face misfortunes and death?

2. The speaker suggests that the person who accepts his or her own mortality but continues "struggling to be/free" (lines 15–16) is the courageous person. It is the struggle that is all important, for the struggle against one's mortality is the struggle to survive. Like "the sea in a chasm," (line 15) one's survival is wholly dependent upon one's resistance to surrender. This struggle will eventually bring joy—the ultimate emotion of human life.

3. A captive, caged bird can continue "his mighty singing" (line 23) for it is in its joyful nature to do so. A person, imprisoned by knowledge of human mortality, must find the courage to behave as heroically as the caged bird behaves. One must also continue "his mighty singing." Only then can an individual recognize eternity, for only then has one behaved heroically and acknowledged the joy within.

4. What are years? They are the opportunity one has to prove oneself capable of making this enormous struggle toward joy. Even though one is imprisoned by human mortality, the years provide the time that courage needs to set an individual free.

Additional Questions

1. Examine the sounds repeated throughout the poem. The first stanza, for example, repeats the "d" sound. What effect does this produce? What sounds are repeated in stanzas two and three? What effect does the repetition have?

   The "d" sounds of stanza one, repeated in "doubt," "dumbly," "deafly," "death," and "defeat," create a tone of seriousness and are spoken in a low voice almost of awe. The second stanza finds tension building through the repetition of "s" sounds in such words as "strong," "sees," "accedes," "imprisonment," "rises," "chasm," and "surrendering." Finally the last stanza is filled with sounds of triumph and joy that are picked up in the "y" sounds of such words as "lovely," "mortality," "eternity."

2. Moore has used paradox (text page 340) most effectively in this poem. Examine lines 4–10, 17–18, and 26–27. What paradoxes are developed in these lines? In what ways is the overall meaning of the poem a paradox?

   The paradox developed in the first stanza revolves around the question of courage. It seems contradictory to suggest that human courage may stem from doubt and unanswered questions. But the paradox is just that. Because of doubt and innocence, an individual struggles and finds a heroism or courage that might not otherwise be acquired. The second paradox is that of a person's survival that is based upon continuing to struggle like the sea, "struggling to be/free and unable to be . . ." (lines 15–16). Thirdly, one's mortality is one's eternity. For in recognizing that an individual is mortal, one struggles heroically; one does not cower or give in to that mere mortality. All of these paradoxes lead to the final paradox of the poem which is inherent in the poem's theme. Although human beings are trapped, they can be at the same time, free. For people have the capability of struggling against mortality until they have found their freedom, the joy of the human spirit.

An Old Woman and Her Cat / p. 417
Doris Lessing (born 1919)

To be old and alone can be a frightening prospect. How a person copes with this experience depends upon the strength of her character. While the old woman in this story may be old and alone, she remains independent and undaunted to the end. Doris Lessing, one of the most gifted writers in the English language today, explores the last years of an old woman's life.

Insight
1. Hetty is a strong woman, a totally independent being, capable of finding her own way in the streets and alleys of London. She feeds herself, clothes herself, finds her own homes. Even while she appeared to be happily married to Pennefather, she had been considered a little strange. After his death and her children's departure, her strange behavior intensified until she became a person totally freed from familial and societal restraints. She no longer saw any reason to pretend to be a part of traditional society. She enjoyed too much a more nomadic, gypsy life of trading and selling. Thus, consciously she rejected the "traditional occupations for middleaged women living alone" (page 418), and took up begging. "Decent people did not beg. She was no longer decent" (page 418).
2. Recognizing her loneliness as she becomes ostracized from former friends and neighbors, Hetty chose Tibby to be her companion. Both Tibby and Hetty display a spirit of independence and a strong will to survive. The cat would go on hunting trips for food; Hetty would go on foraging trips for clothes she would then sell for food. The cat was "a scarred warrior . . . He was a long way down the scale from the delicately coloured, eloquently shaped pedigree cats" (page 419). Hetty, too, as she fights for her survival in the streets of London, becomes a "scarred warrior." She, too, was a colorful creature dressed in her acquired rags, "a long way down the scale" from the aristocracy or even the middle class. As Hetty ages, the cat becomes more and more

important to her very survival. It delivers food, provides warmth. At the same time it is indirectly responsible for Hetty's death by being the factor that keeps her from going to a home. By the end, the cat and Hetty could both illustrate the words the cat catcher speaks to Tibby, "You're an old soldier, aren't you?...A real tough one, a real old tramp" (page 431).

3. While Hetty is healthy, she appears to have a clear understanding of herself. It is only with winter and bad health weakening her that she overestimates her capabilities. Before that she recognizes the "call" of her gypsy blood and realizes that she is happy only when living as freely as she possibly can.

Additional Questions

1. Very little action occurs in this story. Yet the tension builds through the effective use of detail to make the reader see and feel the surroundings in which Hetty finds herself. What details contribute to the feeling of tension in the story? Images of sight, touch, smell, sound, and taste heighten the reader's awareness of Hetty's world. What images do you find particularly strong?

Some students may suggest that the details concerning Tibby contribute to the mounting tension. A young, hungry kitten evolves into an old "scarred warrior." As his bruises and scars mount so does the tension in the story. Other students may suggest that the descriptions of Hetty's various homes create a growing tension. She moves from a crowded council flat in London eventually to an empty house where "for the first time in her life she lived like her gypsy forbears, and did not go to bed in a room in a house like respectable people" (page 423). All the time the reader is aware that life is becoming harder for Hetty. Students may also point to such effective images as the one of Hetty's receiving the pigeons from Tibby and preparing them for a shared dinner, or the images describing Hetty's deteriorating health, or the descriptions of the cat such as "Tibby now looked like a mass of old wool that has been matting together in dust and rain" (page 422).

2. Describe Hetty's relationship with her children. Why won't she turn to them for help? Does she at any time in the story seem resentful of their treatment of her? Cite passages from the story to support your answer.

As Hetty's children left home and found their mother's behavior more and more an embarrassment to them, the relationship between mother and children became almost nonexistent. For some years, Hetty received a Christmas card from one daughter, but even that eventually stopped. Hetty treasured that last card, however, and in her final illness revealed her resentment toward her children as she talked aloud to the card. "I've been a good mother to you...I never let you want for anything, never!" (page 429). Hetty was bitter and angry that her children were not there to help her when she as last needed them. It was her own spirit of independence, however, that had caused her years ago to break from them; it is this same independent spirit that precludes Hetty's going anywhere now for help.

Composition

1. Hetty has lived the last years of her life struggling to maintain the freedom so important to her. Describe her struggle and its outcome. Did her struggle have a meaning or was it merely the perversity of a stubborn old woman?
2. Describe an incident in your own life in which the natural elements were a major factor. For example, you might describe sailing during a storm, walking in the rain, driving in the fog. Try to re-create the atmosphere through the use of detail and imagery.

Thanking My Mother for Piano Lessons / p. 432
Diane Wakoski (born 1937)

With particularly brilliant and memorable images, Wakoski explains in this poem her rather ambivalent feelings toward piano lessons specifically and life generally.

Insight

1. With clear understanding, the speaker describes herself as having been "a quiet child" (line 41) afraid of much of life. Her fears and insecurities were so deep that she felt she lived in "a loveless world" (line 60). As an adult many of her insecurities still exist, but she has been able to pick some love "like lint, out of the corners of pockets" (line 115). She holds desperately to that love for it "stops from pounding, banging,/battering through my brain," (lines 126–127) the memories and meaning of all those years of piano lessons.
2. The hours spent playing the piano and the recognition the speaker gained as a young girl cloaked her feelings of ugliness, of insecurity, of loneliness. An unhappy "timid little life" (line 107) could be buried in hours of practicing, in "the relief of putting your fingers on the keyboard" (line 1). She became someone worthy of attention and praise, but mostly she escaped her loneliness and her own image of an inadequate, ugly self. As an adult, the speaker has forsaken the piano for it too clearly symbolizes to her the ugly past she wants to forget. But the memories of that past cannot be totally quieted for the "painfully loud/music" (lines 124–125) is hushed only by the love of a man.

Additional Questions

1. What kind of person was the speaker's mother? How would you describe the life she led?

    The speaker's mother was a poor, but hard-working, self-sacrificing woman. Her lonely existence is epitomized in her bed that "she slept on only one side of,/never wrinkling an inch of/the other side,/waiting,/waiting" (lines 70–74).

2. Wakoski's poetry is full of rich imagery. Which images did you find particularly effective?

   Few lines of Wakoski's poem do not contain some particularly stunning imagery. Some students, however, might mention lines such as "clean shining Republican middle-class hair" (line 21) or "a world of dime-store purchases" (line 58). Other students may point to the various descriptions of the speaker's mother or the description of "what little love I've been able to/pick, like lint, out of the corners of pockets" (lines 114–115).

Composition

The speaker of the poem talks "of the beauty that can come/from even an ugly/past." Discuss this statement either in terms of the poem itself or in terms of an experience from your own life.

from **A Room of One's Own** / **p. 436**
Virginia Woolf (1882–1941)

The brilliant writer of fiction and essays Virginia Woolf explores in this selection why men have been the intellectual creators and great wielders of power and influence while women historically have been regarded as uncreative and powerless.

Insight

1. Woolf incorporates her answers in her illustration contrasting the two colleges, Oxbridge and Fernham. Fernham offers no "room of one's own" for its students. It does not have the "amenities" nor the tradition that create a comfortable, dignified learning environment. Women have not been offered the facilities, physical and intellectual, that men have so long taken for granted. How, then, can society expect of women a Shakespeare or a Shaw if it deprives a woman of her proper share of the physical, cultural, and traditional "amenities"? After merely beef and prunes what woman has heart left for "exploring or writing; mooning about the venerable places of the earth; sitting contemplative on the steps of the Parthenon, or going at ten to an office and coming home comfortably at half-past four to write a little poetry"? (page 446).

2. It is because she is a woman that she is turned onto the gravel path rather than allowed to walk the turf; it is because she is a woman that she is turned away from the library. The main experience of the day, however, is her sharing of the luncheon with the university scholars. This experience stands in strong contrast to her later dinner at Fernham.

3. The meal at Oxbridge is a sumptuous display of bounty and wealth. Wines, red and white, partridges, fish, roasts are all served. The meal is served with style and dignity. It was a meal over which one would take time to ponder the meaning of life, for it was a meal which fed "the seat of the soul," that is, the intellectual and spiritual side of one's existence. "How good life seemed, how sweet its rewards, how trivial this grudge or that grievance, how admirable friendship and the society of one's kind . . ." (page 442). The meal at Fernham, on the other hand, was a homely combination of beef, potatoes and greens. There was no style, no grandeur. "There was nothing to stir the fancy . . ." Certainly the meal was adequate for physical well-being, but it was totally inadequate for the spiritual and intellectual well-being so necessary for creative endeavors. It is simply that beef and prunes do not create a sense of well-being; they do not encourage, Woolf implies, the feeling that life is sweet and grudges trivial. The women at Fernham have been denied not only the food but the rich tradition that exists for the men at Oxbridge. To deny women both the nourishment for the "seat of the soul" and the tradition is to deny them the opportunity to fulfill their spiritual and intellectual selves.

4. As contrasted with richly endowed Oxbridge, with its traditions of learning and elegance, Fernham was built upon the small pledges of many hard-working people. Just to get thirty thousand pounds with which to start the college was an incredible struggle. As a result, there was never enough money for the amenities, sofas, or separate rooms, or fancy dishes, or pleasurable meals. And even if suddenly the money were there, still missing would be the five centuries of foundation underlying the college. These five centuries have provided a wealth of tradition and background which Fernham shall always lack.

5. Woolf is really pondering the question of woman's ability to escape her traditional role and to demand a place of her own. The effect of poverty Woolf has seen at Fernham. It is hard for her to believe that a woman can produce to her intellectual capacity under the deprived conditions in which she must study there. The question is even larger. Can a woman fulfill her intellectual capabilities under economically deprived conditions? Why must women face obstacles that men have never encountered? Even the simple comforts of life have been denied women as they attempt to develop themselves. As Woolf says, "The deep armchairs and the pleasant carpets . . . the urbanity, the geniality, the dignity which are the off-spring of luxury and privacy and space" (page 447) are stimulating and nice, indeed.

Additional Questions

1. "A woman must have money and a room of her own if she is to write fiction," declares Woolf. How does she demonstrate this need in the

selection? Why do you suppose she calls this need a "minor point"? Do you agree with her? Explain.

Many students will probably agree that this is, indeed, a minor point when contrasted with the larger questions of the true nature of woman and the true nature of fiction. Some students may suggest that Woolf implies, however, that before examining the greater issues, the "minor point" must be pondered for herein lies the beginning of the larger answer. As Woolf begins to illustrate the effect of lack of money and a room of one's own upon women, she clarifies the difficulty women face. For example, in her contrasts of the meals at the Oxbridge and Fernham colleges, Woolf epitomizes the differences in the two colleges. As she says, ". . . a good dinner is of great importance to good talk. One cannot think well, love well, sleep well, if one has not dined well" (page 444). How then can these women at Fernham exercise their full intellectual powers on beef and prunes? Further, Woolf points out that women have been conspired against by men for generations. The traditions and conventions that men have always accepted, enjoyed, and been inspired by have been denied women. To write, a woman must have confining obstacles removed. Then she, like her male counterpart, will have a full and richly endowed background from which to draw.

2. What possible meanings does Woolf state may be attached to the title "women and fiction"? What is the "fatal drawback" to considering the three possible meanings together?

Woolf enumerates the following possible meanings: 1. what women and fiction are like; 2. the fiction written by women; 3. the fiction that is written about women; 4. or all three "inextricably mixed together." The fatal drawback is one's inability to draw a conclusion. Discussing any of the above points leaves unsolved "the great problem of the true nature of woman and the true nature of fiction" (page 436).

3. What is the significance to Oxbridge of the "unending stream of gold and silver"? Why do the narrator's thoughts return to "a scene of masons on a high roof some five centuries ago"?

The "unending stream of gold and silver" represents the unending offers of wealth and the rich cultural and traditional backgrounds that go to build the school, to endow the school, and to inspire those studying at the school. The stream of gold and silver continues to pour in through the centuries and to build a greater and finer institution. The narrator is obsessed with the scene of masons because they symbolize a venerable institution, built by kings and princes and maintained in its original majesty, a majesty denied to women. Speaking of Fernham, she says, "what lies beneath its gallant red brick and the wild unkempt grasses of the garden? What force is behind the plain china off which we dined, and (here it popped out of my mouth before I could stop it) the beef, the custard and the prunes?" (page 494). The contrast between the glory of Oxbridge and the poverty of Fernham is representative to Woolf of the obstacles placed in women's way.

4. For what reason does Woolf appear initially to condemn "Mrs. Seton and her mother and her mother"? What "snag" does she soon recognize in her position?

Woolf initially wonders where these women were when a college needed building. Why did they not, like their male counterparts, endow a school, build it, and maintain it? Why did not the Mrs. Setons have money to spend on such a cause? "What had our mothers been doing then that they had no wealth to leave us? Powdering their noses? Looking in at shop windows?" (page 445). Why had these mothers not gone into business as their husbands had? Then there would have been money to leave to worthy causes of their choosing. But there is a snag in the argument. For Woolf realizes that had these women gone to work there would have been no children and no meaningful family life to look back upon. Thus there would have been no need for any kind of college. "For, to endow a college would necessitate the suppression of families altogether. Making a fortune and bearing thirteen children —no human being could stand it," (page 446) Woolf facetiously comments.

Composition

1. How would you explain Woolf's reflections, "I thought how unpleasant it is to be locked out; and I thought how it is worse to be locked in"? What do you think is the effect of each condition "upon the mind of a writer"? What is the effect of each condition upon any individual?

2. What does Woolf mean when she states "Lies will flow from my lips, but there may perhaps be some truth mixed up with them; it is for you to seek out this truth and to decide whether any part of it is worth keeping." What "lies" does she tell? What "truth" did you find "mixed up with them"? Why do you suppose Woolf felt she could best make her point by telling "lies" in order to tell the "truth"?

In Summary

Breaking free from one's parents, or one's background, or one's superstitions, or one's love is never easy nor is the commonness of the deed any comfort to the individual attempting the break. It must often be done and so it is done and so it has long been done.

Perhaps growing up itself is but a series of small breaking frees: that first day at school, that realization that Santa Claus doesn't really exist, that move to a strange city, that new job. So many breaking frees in a lifetime that we should all be experts in the act. Yet to an old woman long dependent on a dominant, vivacious sister, the act fails despite the clear purpose. But, a young bride trapped by a moment of reality astounds even herself as she learns that she can and must break free from what she has been taught to be.

Breaking free guarantees nothing. To be free finally from the Liberty School may be to settle into another school much the same. To be free and a leader in a social movement may bring one fame, but will not necessarily assure immortality. To break free from a fifteen year engagement is but to set one's course in another pattern.

While to attempt to break free may assure nothing of substance, the act itself—successful or not—serves to free the spirit.

Suggested Reading

*Baez, Joan. *Daybreak*. New York: Dial Press, 1968.

*Brontë, Charlotte. *Villette*. Boston: Houghton Mifflin, 1971.

Didion, Joan. *Slouching Towards Bethlehem*. New York: Farrar, Straus & Giroux, 1968.

Dinesen, Isak. *Seven Gothic Tales*. New York: Random House, 1972.

*Glasgow, Ellen. *Barren Ground*. New York: Hill & Wang, 1957.

*——. *Collected Stories*. Louisiana: Louisiana State University Press, 1966.

Grau, Shirley. *The Black Prince and Other Stories*. New York: Alfred A. Knopf, 1955.

Lessing, Doris. *Children of Violence*. New York: Simon and Schuster, 1964–66.

——. *The Golden Notebook*. New York: Simon and Schuster, 1962.

*Millay, Edna St. Vincent. *Collected Poems*. New York: Harper and Row, 1956.

*Murray, Michele. *The Crystal Nights*. New York: Seabury Press, 1973.

* Richardson, Dorothy. *Pilgramage*. New York: Alfred A. Knopf, 1967.

*Teasdale, Sara. *Collected Poems of Sara Teasdale*. New York: Macmillan, 1967.

Undset, Sigrid. *Kristin Lavransdatter*. New York: Alfred A. Knopf, 1935.

Wakoski, Diane. *The Motorcycle Betrayal Poems*. New York: Simon and Schuster, 1971.

*Walker, Margaret. *In Love and Trouble: Stories of Black Women:* New York: Harcourt Brace Jovanovich, 1974.

*West, Jessamyn. *Hide and Seek*. New York: Harcourt Brace Jovanovich, 1973.

Wharton, Edith. *The Age of Innocence*. New York: Scribner's, 1968.

Woolf, Virginia. *Mrs. Dalloway*. New York: Harcourt Brace Jovanovich, 1949.

——. *To the Lighthouse*. New York: Harcourt Brace Jovanovich, 1949.

bibliography

The following books are suggested as resource material for your own use. You may find, however, that some of the material in these collections is suitable for classroom use.

Bernikow, Louise, ed. *The World Split Open: Four Centuries of Women Poets in England and America, 1552–1950.* New York: Vintage Books, 1974.

Chester, Laura, and Barba Sharon, eds. *Rising Tides: 20th Century American Women Poets.* New York: Pocket Books, 1973.

Edwards, Lee R., and Arlyn Diamond, eds. *American Voices, American Women.* New York: Avon Books, 1973.

Ferguson, Mary Anne, ed. *Images of Women in Literature.* Boston: Houghton Mifflin, 1973.

Goulianos, Joan, ed. *By a Woman Writt: Literature from Six Centuries by and about Women.* Baltimore: Penguin Books, 1974.

Howe, Florence, and Ellen Bass, eds. *No More Masks: An Anthology of Poems by Women.* New York: Anchor Press, 1973.

Murray, Michele, ed. *A House of Good Proportion: Images of Women in Literature.* New York: Simon and Schuster, 1973.

Schulman, L. M., ed. *A Woman's Place.* New York: Macmillan, 1974.

Segnitz, Barbara, and Carol Rainey, eds. *Psyche: The Feminine Poetic Consciousness.* New York: Dell, 1973.

Stanford, Ann, ed. *The Women Poets in English.* New York: McGraw-Hill, 1972.

NOTES